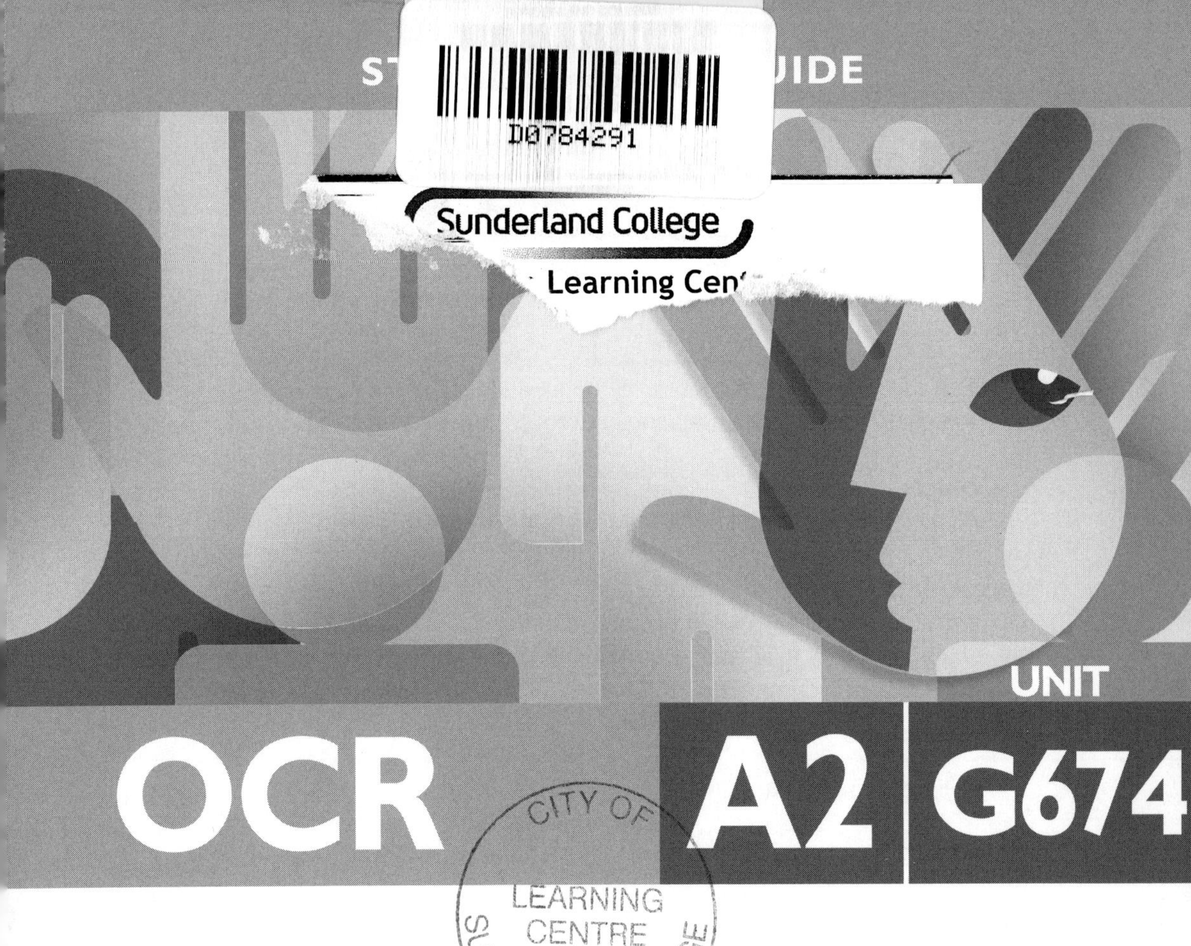

ST… …UIDE

UNIT

OCR A2 G674

Sociology

Exploring Social Inequality and Difference

Steve Chapman

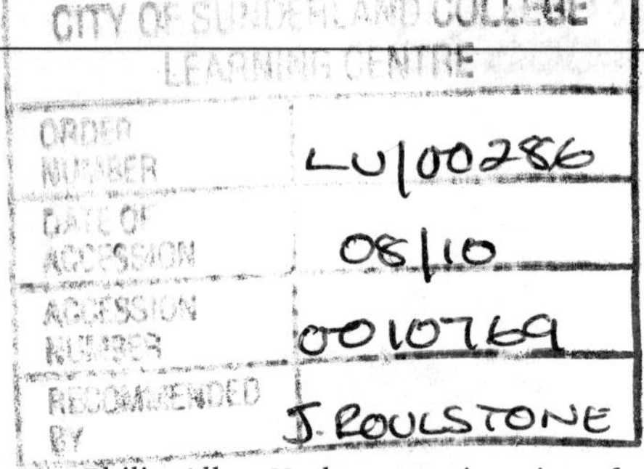

Philip Allan Updates, an imprint of Hodder Education, an Hachette UK company, Market Place, Deddington, Oxfordshire OX15 0SE

Orders

Bookpoint Ltd, 130 Milton Park, Abingdon, Oxfordshire, OX14 4SB
tel: 01235 827720
fax: 01235 400454
e-mail: uk.orders@bookpoint.co.uk
Lines are open 9.00 a.m.–5.00 p.m., Monday to Saturday, with a 24-hour message answering service. You can also order through the Philip Allan Updates website: www.philipallan.co.uk

ISBN 978-0-340-96675-4

First printed 2009
Impression number 5 4 3 2
Year 2013 2012 2011 2010

This guide has been written specifically to support students preparing for the OCR A2 Sociology Unit G674 examination. The content has been neither approved nor endorsed by OCR and remains the sole responsibility of the author.

Typeset by Phoenix Photosetting, Chatham, Kent
Printed by MPG Books, Bodmin

Hachette UK's policy is to use papers that are natural, renewable and recyclable products and made from wood grown in sustainable forests. The logging and manufacturing processes are expected to conform to the environmental regulations of the country of origin.

P01471

Contents

Questions and Answers

Introduction

This unit guide is for students following the OCR A2 Sociology course. It deals with Unit G674 **Exploring Social Inequality and Difference**, which covers sociological theories, concepts and evidence relating to the underlying processes that shape the life chances of individuals in contemporary Britain. This unit demands a strong knowledge of the relationship between social inequality and difference relating to gender, class, ethnicity and age and methods of sociological enquiry, i.e. the research tools that might be used to investigate these.

This module is synoptic, which means you will use theories, concepts and evidence about social inequality and difference that you have studied in other units, such as the AS units on **Exploring Socialisation, Culture and Identity** and topics such as family, health, religion and youth and topics from A2 Unit G673 **Power and Control**, e.g. crime and deviance, education, mass media and power and politics.

This guide has three sections:

- **Introduction** — advice on how to use this guide, an explanation of the skills required in A2 Sociology, suggestions for effective revision and guidance on how to succeed in the unit test.
- **Content Guidance** — an outline of what is included in the specification for this unit. It is designed to make you aware of what you need to know before the unit examination.
- **Questions and Answers** — mock exam questions for you to try, together with some sample answers at grade-A and grade-C level, with examiner's comments on how the marks are awarded.

How to use the guide

The Introduction and Content Guidance sections of this guide can be referred to from the beginning of your study of **Exploring Social Inequality and Difference**. Leave the Question and Answer section until you have completed your study of the topic, as the questions are wide-ranging. When you are ready to use this section, you should take each question in turn, study it carefully, and write a full answer yourself. Then study the grade-A candidate's answer and compare it with your own, paying close attention to the examiner's comments. Another strategy is to look first at the grade-C answer and, using the examiner's comments as a guide, rewrite it to gain higher marks.

The A2 specification

This specification aims to encourage you to:

- acquire knowledge and a critical understanding of contemporary social processes and social changes

- appreciate the significance of theoretical and conceptual issues in sociological debate
- understand and evaluate sociological methodology and a range of research methods through active involvement in the research process
- develop skills that enable individuals to focus on their personal identity, roles and responsibilities within society
- develop a lifelong interest in social issues
- show an understanding of the links between the nature of sociological thought, the methods of sociological enquiry and the core themes of power, social inequality, socialisation, culture and identity
- think holistically and develop skills of thinking as a sociologist

Examinable skills

The three main examinable skills in the A2 specifications are divided into two **Assessment Objectives**.

Assessment Objective 1

AO1: **knowledge and understanding** (46% of total A2 marks)

You should demonstrate:

- wide-ranging, detailed knowledge of relevant sociological theories, concepts, methods and different types of evidence, especially statistical data and empirical studies; holistic understanding of how different areas relate to the topic
- a clear understanding of what you are describing, beyond learning by rote; an ability to discuss the merits of particular arguments in an organised fashion
- learning and using relevant knowledge about the topic, including the main arguments, the sociologists who have contributed to the debate, the concepts they used and the historical context . You should also be familiar with empirical studies and data supporting or undermining the arguments.

Assessment Objective 2

AO2 (a): **interpretation and analysis** (27% of total A2 marks); AO2 (b) **evaluation** (27% of total A2 marks)

For **interpretation and analysis**, you should demonstrate:

- the ability to select and analyse different types of evidence and data
- the ability to apply and link sociological evidence to specific sociological arguments
- the ability to interpret quantitative and qualitative data, including identifying relevant knowledge, distinguishing between fact and opinion, identifying patterns and trends in data

For **evaluation**, you should demonstrate:

- the ability to assess the validity of sociological arguments and the available evidence and data in a balanced way
- the ability to examine the reliability of the methods used to collect evidence, and assess its validity

Whenever you are introduced to a sociological perspective or study, you should evaluate it by finding at least three criticisms that have been made of it, whether these are specific criticisms of the theory and its supporting evidence or its methods of data collection, or alternative theories that can be used as a point of contrast. However, you will need to assess the worth of the criticisms and use only those that make sense according to the sociological context, providing a balanced evaluation.

Study skills and revision strategies

Keep your sociology folder in good order from the start, as it is an important revision aid. Go back over your essays and exam answers, read your teacher's comments, and see whether you can redo any pieces that did not score good marks.

Use a separate part of your folder and write down the definition of a concept when you first come across it. Make a brief summary of research studies, particularly those not found in your textbook. Remember to include the title, author(s) and, most importantly, the date, along with your summary of the method(s) used and the main findings. Keep these in a section in your sociology folder, or record them on index cards.

Practise writing answers within the time limit, making sure you have time not only to complete all the parts of the question, but also to reread and correct your answer.

Comprehensive revision is not something that can be done the night before the exam. Visit the website **www.getrevising.co.uk** — it will help you put together a practical and realistic revision timetable.

Aim to do 90 minutes of revision per evening from Monday to Thursday, take Friday night off, and do 3 hours of revision over the weekend. It is a good idea to revise in concentrated bursts of time. Take a break after 45 minutes, and then switch to a different topic for variety. During the weekend revision session, try answering a question under timed conditions.

The unit examination

Exploring Social Inequality and Difference is the only Unit G674 topic. The unit examination is composed of two **compulsory questions** focused on sociological research worth 40 marks. You then choose one of **options 1 and 2**, which contain two questions each on a specific aspect of social inequality and difference worth 60 marks altogether. The examination lasts 2 hours.

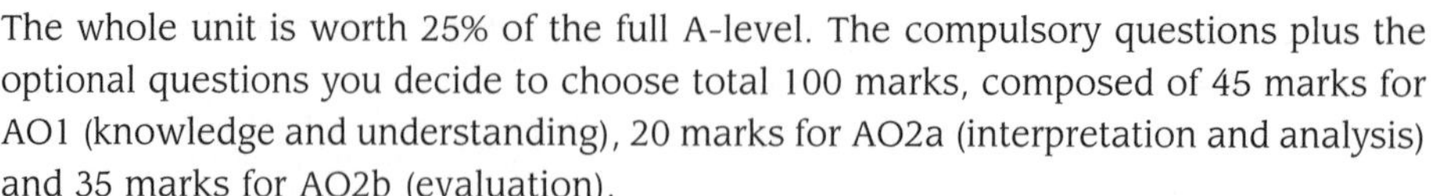

The whole unit is worth 25% of the full A-level. The compulsory questions plus the optional questions you decide to choose total 100 marks, composed of 45 marks for AO1 (knowledge and understanding), 20 marks for AO2a (interpretation and analysis) and 35 marks for AO2b (evaluation).

The question will contain one piece of extended source material. It is essential that you spend some time carefully reading through this material because its content is aimed to give you clues as to the direction your responses might take. The source material can be actively used in your response.

Compulsory question 1 (15 marks: 10 AO1 marks, 5 AO2 marks) asks you to use the specimen material and your own knowledge to describe and explain how a particular research method or approach might be used in sociological research. Spend about 20 minutes on this question, including time for reading the specimen material.

Compulsory question 2 (25 marks: 15 AO2b marks, 5 AO1 marks, 5 AO2a marks) asks you to describe and assess a particular research method or approach, and is likely to be linked to the subject matter in the specimen material. Most of the marks available are for evaluation, so focus on assessing the reliability of the method or approach in terms of its strengths and weaknesses, and its validity in terms of the type of data it is likely to produce. Spend about 30 minutes on this question.

Options 1 and 2: choose between two options each containing two questions; **Option 1**, question 3 (a) and 3 (b) OR Option 2; question 4 (a) and 4 (b). Be careful here not to make the mistake of doing all the questions in both options, neither must you mix and match questions from both options; choose one or the other.

Question 3 (a) or 4 (a) (20 marks: 15 AO1 marks, 5 AO2a marks): a synoptic question that asks you to outline or describe evidence from sociological studies and/or statistical data which supports the view that some social groups experience social inequalities and differences relating to social class, gender, age and ethnicity. This evidence may be taken from what you have learned specifically as part of the Exploring Social Inequality and Difference module, but it should be supplemented by evidence from other units. These might be from your AS units or from the Power and Control topic you will have studied at A2. While revising for this question you must build up a 'synoptic store' of evidence to draw on.

Most of the marks for this question are for knowledge and understanding. There are no marks for evaluation and analysis — you do not have to show opposing or challenging evidence. Very importantly, you do not have to explain why this evidence has come about. Spend about 25 minutes on this question.

Question 3 (b) or 4 (b) (40 marks: 15 AO1 marks, 20 AO2b marks, 5 AO2a marks): an essay question often containing the words 'assess' or 'evaluate' or 'discuss'. The question is likely to focus on explanations and theories for social inequalities and differences, with the emphais on assessing or evaluating these. You will need to weigh up the strengths and weaknesses (i.e. criticisms) or discuss the advantages and disadvantages of particular theories and explanations. However, it is extremely important that you describe a theory before you begin to assess its merits. This question tests all three skills.

It is important that you develop the skill of writing essays under timed conditions. Begin your essay with an introduction that sets the scene, explaining the point of view contained in the question, defining any technical terms used in the essay title and identifying key sociologists or theories involved in the debate.

You should then explain the view embodied in the question by outlining the key features of particular sociological positions. A good approach is to first outline the theoretical argument(s) and then support these with empirical sociological studies or statistical data. Remember to clearly link whatever you are discussing to the question.

Having outlined and supported the view contained in the question, you can address the evaluation of that view. More marks are allocated to this skill, so your critical appraisal must be fairly substantial. You could begin by addressing specific features of the theories/studies/data already discussed which you think are problematic. The key here is to make sure that the examiner knows you are engaged in evaluation, so use evaluative words or phrases, e.g. 'however' or 'in contrast with'.

You should next outline any alternative theories (with supporting evidence) that challenge the view in the question. Make sure that you clearly state how these alternatives challenge the previous position.

Finally, there are two types of conclusion to choose from. The first is a summative conclusion, which merely reminds the examiner of the competing positions and how they generally differ. But you may prefer the second, an evaluative conclusion, in which you make a judgement based on the evidence as to which position is the most convincing argument. Spend about 45 minutes on this question and aim to fill at least four sides of your answer book.

Content Guidance

This section is intended to show you the major issues and themes covered in **Exploring Social Inequality and Difference**. However, it is not an exhaustive or comprehensive list of the concepts, issues and sociological studies that you could use to answer questions on this topic. Rather, it is an outline of the key concepts that you need to know plus guidance on some issues and sociological studies that are worth further investigation. You should be able to access further information by consulting your teacher, and by using your textbook and past copies of *Sociology Review*.

The content of **Social Inequality and Difference** falls into four main areas:

- patterns and trends of inequality and difference related to social class, gender, ethnicity and age and how these intersect
- theoretical explanations for inequality and difference
- sociological explanations of the changing class structure of UK society
- the research methods useful to sociologists for the social investigation of inequality and difference

The topic is designed to give you an understanding of the underlying processes which shape the life chances and social identities of specific social groups, and in particular the inequality that tends to characterise relationships between different social classes, between men and women, between ethnic groups and between age groups. It also examines how these inequalities might be related to and even caused by the social organisation of contemporary Britain. It is therefore important that we examine wider structural influences, such as the changing class structure and how this might be underpinned by changes in the nature of work and the economy. It is also important to examine the impact of ideology, patriarchy, institutional racism and ageism on culture and identity. Finally, it is essential to understand the constraints that impact on individual social action and choice, especially in regard to wealth, income, poverty and people's relative life chances in education and health.

Patterns and trends of inequality and difference

Defining stratification

It is important to be aware of three key aspects of the unit when you begin your revision. You need to have:

- a detailed knowledge of, and ability to apply accurately, the concepts and theories that underpin the central topic areas in this unit, and to support them, whenever possible, with empirical sociological studies
- evaluative understanding of concepts, theories and studies; evaluation as a skill is highly rewarded at this level
- a 'synoptic awareness', that is, to know how evidence from other topic areas across both the AS and A2 units might be used to support the view that class, gender, ethnic and age inequalities exist

Social stratification

- Social stratification means the division of society into a pattern of layers or strata made up of a hierarchy of unequal social groups.
- In societies characterised by stratification, normally one or two groups dominate the others, and these societies consequently contain inequalities in factors such as wealth and income, occupation and status, social class, political power, religion, race, gender and age.
- Sociologists have identified four types of stratification systems that have existed throughout history, some of which still exist today. These are the caste system, the feudal estate system, the apartheid system and social class.
- The social stratification system found in modern industrial societies, such as the UK, is based on social class.

Concepts of class

- Social classes are groups of people who share a similar economic position through occupation, income and ownership of wealth, as well as having similar levels of education, status, lifestyle (i.e. living standards) and power.
- Class systems are not based on religion or law or race, but on economic factors such as jobs and money.
- In class systems there is no clear distinction between classes. For example, it is difficult to say where the working class ends and the middle class begins.
- All members of societies with class systems, whether working or middle or upper classes, enjoy equal rights.
- There are no legal restrictions on marriage between members of different social groups in societies characterised by class.

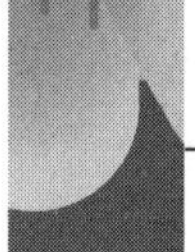

- Class societies are open societies in that people can experience downward or upward social mobility, i.e. they can move up or down the class structure through jobs, the acquisition of wealth or marriage.
- Class systems are supposed to be meritocratic, i.e. people are encouraged to better themselves through achievement at school, and at work through working hard and gaining promotion.

Defining and measuring social class

- Occupation is the most common measure of social class used by governments, by advertising agencies doing market research, and by sociologists when undertaking social surveys.
- Occupation is generally a good guide to people's skills and qualifications, their income, their future prospects and their standard of living in terms of their housing, acquisition of consumer goods etc.
- Occupation usually shapes status in modern society, i.e. most people judge their social standing and that of others by the jobs they do.

The Registrar-General's scale of occupations

The Registrar-General's (RG) scale was used by the government until 2000 to categorise people into social classes in the UK.

The RG scale divided the population into five broad social classes:

- **Class I:** Professional, e.g. accountants, doctors, solicitors
- **Class II:** Intermediate, e.g. teachers, managers, pilots, farmers
- **Class III NM:** Skilled non-manual, e.g. office workers, shop assistants
- **Class III M:** Skilled manual, e.g. electricians, plumbers, factory foremen
- **Class IV:** Semi-skilled manual, e.g. agricultural workers, postal workers
- **Class V:** Unskilled manual, e.g. road sweepers, labourers, refuse collectors

Classes I, II and III NM were generally categorised as middle class, and workers in these categories included professionals, managers and white-collar workers.

Classes III M, IV and V were generally categorised as working class, and workers in these categories were often referred to as blue-collar workers.

The RG scale was used from 1911 and therefore allowed sociologists and social policy makers to compare social change over a period of time.

Evaluation

- The RG scale did not include those members of the wealthy upper class who did not have jobs but instead lived off inherited wealth, or the income from rents or stocks and shares.
- People who did not have paid jobs were excluded, such as housewives and the never-employed/unemployed.

- Classifying people into a social class on the basis of their jobs assumed that they had similar incomes, status, lifestyles etc., but this was often not the case. For example, Social Class I included doctors, but this group encompassed highly paid surgeons and poorly paid junior doctors.
- The RG scale classed families using the job of the 'head of the household'. The RG assumed without question that this was the father or husband. Married women therefore were classified on the basis of their husbands' occupations rather than their own. This system was not only sexist but dated as women went out to work in large numbers and had careers of their own.
- The focus on the head of the household neglected those families in which both partners are important in bringing home a wage (dual-career families). Their joint incomes often give them the lifestyle of a higher class.
- The RG scale did not consider cross-class families in which the female has a higher-paid job and status than the male.
- The RG scale failed to consider the increasing number of single working women and single working mothers, because it determined their social class with reference to their fathers or ex-husbands.

Key concepts

stratification; caste system; feudalism; apartheid; social class; social mobility; meritocratic; ascribed and achieved roles; status; working class; middle class

The National Statistics–Socioeconomic Classification (NS–SEC)

The RG scale was finally abandoned because it failed to reflect the massive decline in manufacturing, the huge growth in service industries (finance and retail) and the large increase in the proportion of women in the workforce.

In 2000, the RG scale was replaced by the National Statistics–Socioeconomic Classification (NS–SEC) devised by John Goldthorpe. This is also based on employment.

It differs from the RG scale in that it is no longer based purely on skill. It is based on:
(a) employment relations, i.e. whether people are employers, self-employed, employed, whether they exercise authority etc., and
(b) employment or market conditions, i.e. salary scales, promotion prospects, sick pay, how much control people have over hours worked or how work is done

The NS–SEC recognises eight social classes rather than five:
(1) higher managerial and professional occupations
(2) lower managerial and professional occupations
(3) intermediate occupations
(4) small employers and own-account workers
(5) lower supervisory, craft and related occupations
(6) semi-routine occupations
(7) routine occupations
(8) long-term unemployed or the never-worked

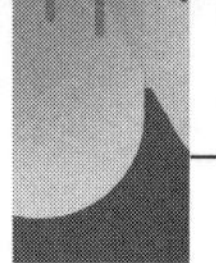

The NS–SEC no longer divides workers along manual and non-manual lines. Each category contains both manual and non-manual workers.

Class 8 is essentially the 'underclass', which the RG scale did not cater for because of its emphasis on occupation.

Occupations such as check-out assistants and sales assistants, who used to be in Class III NM, have been dropped to Class 6 because of their relatively poor conditions of employment (their market situation has deteriorated in terms of pay, job security, autonomy etc.)

Teachers have been promoted from Social Class II to Class 1, higher professionals, because their market position has improved in terms of pay etc.

The self-employed are recognised as a separate category for the first time.

Women are recognised as a distinct group of wage earners and are no longer categorised according to the occupations of their husbands or fathers.

Evaluation

+ The NS–SEC has taken into consideration changing class boundaries, e.g. the fact that the social position of clerical workers has declined.
- The NS–SEC classification is still primarily based on occupation, and this may differ from people's subjective interpretation of their class position.
- There are still significant differences within occupations, e.g. GPs and junior doctors are paid considerably less than consultants.
- It still fails to account for those wealthy enough not to have to work.

Key concepts

employment relations; market conditions; underclass

Patterns of social inequality: social class

The changing nature of the economy

The occupational structure (the organisation of work into full-time employed, part-time employed, unemployed and so on, as well as categories of skill and authority, such as professional, managerial, white-collar, skilled, semi-skilled and unskilled manual work) has changed over time. A number of trends can be seen:

- Between 1986 and 1997, the number of people in jobs rose from 26.9 million to 27.9 million, because more women entered the labour market.
- However, the primary sector (e.g. heavy industries such as coal-mining and shipbuilding) and the secondary sector (e.g. manufacturing or factory work) of the economy have both gone into decline because of worldwide recession and globalisation — the same raw materials and goods can be produced more cheaply in the developing world.

- Male manual work has gone into decline and it is no longer guaranteed that the male will be the main earner in households.
- The tertiary or service sector of the economy (mainly personal services, state services such as education and welfare, and retail and finance) has expanded in the past 20 years because mass secondary education and the expansion of further and higher education have created a well-educated and qualified workforce.
- Many tertiary sector jobs have gone to women, which has prompted some commentators to suggest that the economy has been feminised.
- Ritzer developed the idea of 'McDonaldisation', where global companies develop networks of technologies, skills, brands etc. to ensure that in every country more or less the same product is manufactured and delivered in the same way. He argues that this technique of organising work applies to many parts of the service sector. It is likely to produce new kinds of low-skilled, low-paid, standardised jobs ('McJobs'), especially for young people.
- There has been a movement towards the casualisation of the labour force, e.g. there has been an increase in non-standard contracts. Just under one-third of employees in the late 1990s were part-time or temporary.
- The deterioration of the labour market has had a severe effect upon men, especially young men, who are now more likely to be unemployed and less likely to be in continuous, long-term and stable work.
- Some sociologists argue that the idea of 'a job for life' will soon be a thing of the past.

The effects of workplace change on social class inequalities

A number of observations can be made concerning the distribution of income between 1945 and 2008:

- Between 1979 and 1997, income inequality between the rich and poor widened until it was at its greatest since records began at the end of the nineteenth century. This was because the top rate of income tax was lowered, VAT increased from 8% to 17.5%, and there were large salary rises for 'fat-cat' business leaders.
- Between 1979 and 1992, average income rose by 36%, but it rose by 62% for the top 10% of earners, while it fell by 17% for the poorest 10% of earners.
- The level of inequality in income rose faster in the UK than in any other western nation.
- The Institute for Fiscal Studies' (2008) study of 2007 tax records concluded that income inequality between the rich and the poor is now at its highest level since the late 1940s.
- Since 1997, when Labour took power, income inequality has widened even further: in 2007, the top 0.1% (47,000 people in all) received 4.3% of all income — this was three times greater than their share in 1979. The top 10% of individuals in the UK now receive 40% of all personal income (compared with 21% in 1979) whilst the poorest 10% received only 3% (compared with 4% in 1979).
- The Low Pay Unit argues that low pay is the most important cause of poverty in the UK.

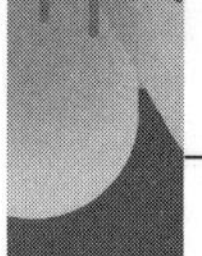

- 45% of British workers are earning less than two-thirds of the average hourly wage.
- Low-paid workers are often caught in a poverty trap, i.e. they earn above the minimum level required to claim benefits, but the deduction of tax etc. takes them below it.
- Low pay also results from the weakening of workers' legal rights and high levels of unemployment, although New Labour introduced a minimum wage policy in 1999.

Synoptic evidence of the continuing importance of social class

Evidence for the continuing importance of social class can be taken from across the specification. Note the word 'evidence'. Statistical trends and patterns and empirical studies count as evidence; pure theory does not. Below are some examples of types of evidence that would support the continuing importance of social class, taken from the fields of health and education. Other areas of the specification, such as the family, media, crime and deviance, and social policy and welfare, can equally provide such evidence (see *Questions and Answers* section).

Social class and health

If illness were a chance occurrence, we would expect to see it randomly distributed across the population. However, some groups can expect disproportionate amounts of illness:

- Working-class people experience poorer mortality and morbidity rates than the middle class. More than 3,500 more working-class babies would survive per year if the working-class infant mortality rate was reduced to middle-class levels.
- If we compare causes of death, we can see that between 1972 and 1993, death rates for professionals from all causes fell by 44%, while the rate fell by only 10% for the unskilled.
- Death rates due to lung cancer among professionals fell by 58%, but the unskilled rate fell by only 25%.
- Death rates due to coronary heart disease fell by 58% among professionals, but the unskilled rate fell by only 3%.
- Working-class people are more likely to die before retirement of cancer, stroke and heart disease than middle-class people.
- There are a number of empirical studies, e.g. Roberts, Wilkinson, Tudor Hart, which attempt through the use of social surveys and official statistics to construct explanations for the poor levels of working-class health, and superior middle-class health, and consequently would count as evidence for use in a part (c) question.

Social class and education

At all stages of education, students from working-class backgrounds achieve less than their middle-class counterparts. Even when working-class children have the same level of intelligence as middle-class children, they are:

- less likely to attend nursery schools or preschool playgroups
- more likely to start school unable to read
- more likely to fall behind in reading, writing and maths skills
- more likely to be placed in lower sets or streams
- more likely to get fewer GCSEs, or low grades
- more likely to leave school at the age of 16
- less likely to go into the sixth form and on to university

A number of empirical studies, e.g. Douglas, Halsey, Wedge and Prosser, Ball, Willis, attempt through the use of social surveys, official statistics and observation to construct explanations for class differences in education, and therefore, their use in part (c) questions counts as evidence.

Social class and poverty

Kempson found that poverty brings about various socioeconomic disadvantages, including:

- debt
- high levels of marital breakdown, especially divorce
- poor diet and nutritional intake, which results in poor immune systems and consequently higher levels of morbidity
- allocation of children to failing schools in inner-city areas
- high levels of educational failure, truancy and exclusion
- allocation to housing estates characterised by crime, drug abuse and unsuitable, deteriorating housing stock
- disproportionate attention from the police, social workers etc.
- newspaper reporting that stereotypes the poor as undeserving and idle welfare scroungers

Treasury figures from March 1999 estimate that up to 25% of children never escape from poverty and that economic deprivation is passed down the generations by underachievement in schools and unemployment.

Sociological and theoretical explanations

Class formation and change

The upper class

A strong and healthy upper class continues to exist in the UK:

- Over the course of the last 100 years, it has changed its character — from being predominantly based on old wealth, i.e. landed gentry and aristocracy who

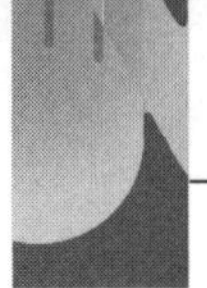

largely inherited their wealth, to being based in the twenty-first century on a combination of old wealth and the wealth of manufacturing, retail and finance.

- Marriage between rich families brought about this amalgamation of old and new wealth.
- Wealth is still the main characteristic of the upper class in 2008.

Overall, the twentieth century saw a gradual redistribution of wealth in the UK:

- In 1911 the richest 1% of the population owned 69% of the wealth, but this had fallen to 18% by 1991.
- However, the redistribution of wealth was very narrow — from the very wealthy (the top 1%) to the wealthy (the top 10%), i.e. to family members in order to avoid paying death duties.
- The result of this redistribution within the economic elite is that in 2003, the top 1% and top 10% owned 18% and 50% of the nation's wealth respectively. 10% owned 50% of the nation's wealth. The wealth of the most affluent 200 individuals and families doubled in 2000.
- In contrast, half the population shared only 10% of total wealth in 1986, and this had been reduced further to 6% by 2003.
- Things look even worse if property ownership is removed from this wealth analysis and the focus is exclusively on wealth in the form of cash, stocks and shares, art and antiques etc. In 2003, the top 1% of the population owned 34% of all personal wealth whilst the bottom 50% owned just 1%.
- Inheritance is still an important source of wealth.
- John Scott points out that the richest 1% of the population own 75% of all privately owned shares. Scott argues that the upper class is a 'unified property class' which owns and controls major sections of the manufacturing, financial (e.g. banks) and retail (e.g. supermarkets) sectors.

However, the amount of wealth concentrated in the hands of the upper class is difficult to estimate for a number of reasons:

- Wealth takes many different forms, such as stocks and shares, capital in banks and building societies, property such as land, housing, cars, antiques and paintings.
- Income tax returns are the main source of information but these are unreliable because the wealthy may not declare their true wealth or income.
- Abercrombie and Warde note that wealth is more concealed than income. Much of it may be in offshore or foreign bank accounts and therefore untraceable.
- Wealthy parents tend to redistribute their assets to children via trust funds before they die in order to avoid inheritance tax.
- Survey research is not very effective in this area because personal wealth is regarded as a private matter.

Kynaston (2008) argues that meritocracy in the UK is undermined by the existence of private schools, which generally reproduce the privileges of the economic elite generation by generation. Only about 7% of all children are educated at private schools, but these pupils take up 45% of Oxbridge places and a disproportionate number at other top UK universities.

The Sutton Trust (2007) ranked the success of schools, over a 5-year period, at getting their pupils into Oxbridge. Top was the Westminster public school, which got 50% of its students into Oxbridge and which charges annual boarding fees of £25,956 for the privilege. This means that the wealthy parents of Westminster pupils have a 50–50 chance of their child making it into Oxbridge. Altogether, there were 27 private schools amongst top 30 schools that have the best Oxbridge record; 43 in the top 50 and 78 in the top 100. The Sutton Trust concluded that the 70th brightest sixth-former at Westminster or Eton is as likely to get a place at Oxbridge as the very brightest sixth-formers at a large comprehensive school.

Scott notes that the upper class or 'establishment' permeate top positions in politics, the civil service, the Church, the armed services and the professions, especially law. Sutton Trust studies show clearly that those in high status jobs, such as senior politicians, top business leaders and judges, are often privately and Oxbridge educated.

Moreover the 'old school tie' network ensures important social contacts for years to come, particularly in the finance sector of the economy. This is, almost certainly, still the most influential pathway to the glittering prizes of top jobs and super-salaries.

The upper class practise social closure, i.e. they use intermarriage, public schools and the old-boy network to ensure that social mobility into the upper class is largely restricted.

Adonis and Pollard (1998) suggest that the upper class has been supplemented by a 'super class' comprising those who have made their fortunes in the City, accountants and managers of investment funds and directors of the former public utilities (water, gas, electricity, British Rail).

Members of this super class tend to intermarry, earn combined super-salaries, and are distinguished from the rest of society by consumption patterns which revolve around nannies and servants, second homes, exotic holidays, private health and pension schemes and private education for their children. Most of the super class live in London and the southeast.

The middle classes

In 1911 80% of workers were in manual occupations (working-class positions). This number fell to 52% in 1981 and to 32.7% in 1991. In the past 10 years, non-manual workers (traditionally seen as middle class) have become the majority occupational group in the workforce because of the shift from primary/secondary types of production to the tertiary or service sector of the economy.

Savage (1995) notes that in 1991, 29.4% of the workforce worked in the professions and management, 10.7% were self-employed and 27.2% were routine white-collar workers. In other words, 67.3% of the working population could be considered as part of the middle class. He argues that it is important to see that the middle class divides into four 'class fractions'.

The self-employed or 'petit-bourgeoisie'

- This group makes up 10% of the workforce.
- The number of managers who prefer to work for themselves, for example as consultants, rose considerably in the 1980s, especially in the finance and computer industries.
- Many firms now prefer to contract services to outside consultants rather than employ people themselves.
- A large number of people, again mainly managers, have businesses on the side while continuing to be employees.
- There are some signs that members of this group of workers, who have traditionally been both conservative and passive in pursuit of their interests, are becoming more militant as they have increasingly become disillusioned with taxation policy.

Professionals

- The position of professional workers (doctors, solicitors, accountants etc.) is based on educational qualifications and a long period of training, i.e. university followed by professional examinations.
- Professionals generally enjoy high economic rewards, status and job security.
- Savage argues that professionals have economic capital (i.e. a very good standard of living and savings) and cultural capital (they see the worth of education and high culture) which they pass on to their children.
- Consequently, Savage et al. argue that the professional sector mainly recruits internally, meaning that the sons and daughters of professionals are likely to end up as professionals themselves.
- Professionals have strong occupational associations that protect and actively pursue their interests (e.g. the Law Society, the British Medical Association) although lower down the professional ladder, these associations/unions become weaker (e.g. teachers' unions).
- Professionals are aware of their common interests and are willing to take collective action to protect those interests.
- Professionals have a greater sense of class identity than other middle-class groups.

Managers

- Savage suggests that managers have assets based upon a particular skill within specific organisations, and these are not easily transferable to other companies or industries.
- Many managers have been upwardly mobile from the routine white-collar sector, or the skilled working class, and consequently they lack qualifications such as degrees.
- Managerial social position is likely to be the result of experience and reputation rather than qualifications.
- Most managers do not belong to professional associations or trade unions. Consequently, they are more individualistic, less likely to identify a common collectivist interest with their fellow managers, and much more likely to see fellow managers as competitors.
- Savage argues that managers encourage their children to pursue higher education because they can see the benefits of a professional career.

- Managers, despite having economic capital (they are well paid), are less likely to have the professionals' cultural capital.
- Savage argues that managers are less likely to have job security than professionals — they are constantly under threat from recession, mergers, downsizing etc.
- Savage points out that middle managers may find themselves unemployed, downwardly mobile into the routine white-collar sector or becoming self-employed rather than becoming higher managers such as company directors.

White-collar workers and proletarianisation

- Marxists, such as Harry Braverman, argue that routine white-collar workers are no longer middle class because they have been subjected to a process of proletarianisation, i.e. they have lost the social and economic advantages that they enjoyed over manual workers, such as superior pay and working conditions.
- Braverman argues that in the past 20 years employers have used technology to break down complex white-collar skills, such as book-keeping, into simplistic routine tasks. This process is known as deskilling and is an attempt to increase output, maximise efficiency and reduce costs.
- These developments have been accompanied by the parallel development of feminising the routine white-collar workforce, especially in the financial sector — female workers are generally cheaper to employ and are seen by employers as more adaptable and amenable.
- Braverman concludes that deskilling means that occupations that were once middle class are now indistinguishable from those of manual workers. Many routine white-collar workers now have similar conditions of work and pay to blue-collar workers.

Evaluation

- Research by Devine suggests that there are still distinct cultural differences in terms of values, lifestyles and political attitudes between manual workers and white-collar workers.
- White-collar workers still generally enjoy advantages at work such as flexitime, fringe benefits, longer holidays and safer working conditions compared with manual workers.
- The NS–SEC recognises that there may be some overlap between white-collar workers and skilled manual workers and therefore does not play up the traditional blue-collar and white-collar distinction in its categorisation of occupations.

The working class

Until the late twentieth century the working class had a strong sense of its social class position. Lockwood's 1966 research found that many workers, especially in industrial areas, subscribed to a value system he called proletarian traditionalist. Workers felt a strong sense of loyalty to each other because of shared work experience. Consequently, workers were mutually supportive and had a keen sense of class

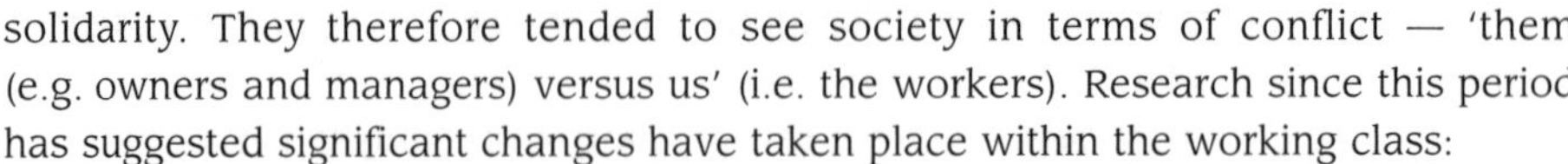

solidarity. They therefore tended to see society in terms of conflict — 'them (e.g. owners and managers) versus us' (i.e. the workers). Research since this period has suggested significant changes have taken place within the working class:

- It was argued in the 1960s by Zweig that a section of the working class, skilled manual workers (the 'labour aristocracy'), had adopted the economic and cultural lifestyle of the middle class. This became known as the embourgeoisement thesis.
- However, Goldthorpe and Lockwood's *Affluent Worker* study in the late 1960s found little evidence to support Zweig's assertion, although they did spot signs of 'convergence' between working-class and middle-class lifestyles.
- Goldthorpe and Lockwood identified the emergence of an instrumental collectivist (sometimes called privatised instrumentalist) worker who saw work as a means to an end rather than as a source of class identity.
- These affluent workers were more home-centred, were less likely to join trade unions or vote Labour, and were found in the newer manufacturing industries mainly situated in the south.
- Instrumental collectivists took industrial action in pursuit of higher pay or to protect living standards relative to other groups of workers, who they perceived as better off, rather than because of a shared class identity.

Evaluation

- Marxists reject the view that there is a fragmented working class and argue that there is a unified working class made up of manual workers, both black and white, male and female, and routine white-collar workers.
- The fact that some groups do not see themselves subjectively as working class is dismissed by Marxists as false class consciousness.
- Marxists argue that in relation to the means and social relations of production, all so-called 'class fractions' are objectively working class because they are alienated and exploited by the ruling class, whether they realise it or not.

Key concepts

the upper class; the establishment; the unified property class; the super class; social closure; petit-bourgeoisie; professionals; economic capital; cultural capital; high culture; the middle classes; class fractions; white-collar workers; proletarianisation; deskilling; collectivistic action; false class consciousness; instrumental collectivism; proletarian traditionalist; embourgeoisement; convergence; labour aristocracy; class solidarity; class identity

The underclass

The underclass thesis separates the underclass from the working class. The New Right version of this theory blames the victim.

- The New Right argues that the underclass is a distinct social group that exists in the inner cities and on council estates. It is made up of the long-term unemployed and those who have never worked. This group supposedly subscribes to a deviant 'way of life' or culture organised around being workshy, benefit dependency, promiscuity and criminality.

- The underclass is allegedly reproduced generation by generation as parents socialise their children into this culture.
- The welfare state is seen as perpetuating such a system because knowledge that benefits are available demotivates people in their search for work.

Evaluation

- The structural view of the underclass rejects the view that most poor people choose not to work. Instead it stresses that structural obstacles, beyond the control of individuals, are responsible for their poverty and encourage fatalism and dependency. Many people are long-term unemployed because of recession or the fact that goods can be produced more cheaply in less economically developed countries.
- Groups such as ethnic minorities may be denied access to jobs and decent housing because of racism.
- Single mothers may find it impossible to return to work because of a lack of free or affordable childcare.
- The underclass is scapegoated for its position at the bottom of the socioeconomic hierarchy.

Is social class dead or declining in importance?

Since the 1990s, postmodernist sociologists have argued that class has ceased to be the prime determinant of identity and that societies today are organised around consumption rather than production. Consequently, people identify themselves in terms of what they consume rather than by social class.

- Postmodernists argue that class identity has fragmented into numerous individualised identities. Pakulski and Waters (1996) argue that people exercise more choice about the type of people they want to be, their identity no longer automatically constructed by social class.
- Postmodernists argue that gender, ethnicity, age, region and family role all interact with consumption and media images to construct postmodern culture and identity.

Evaluation

- Marshall's survey indicates that social class is still a significant source of identity, and that people are often aware of class differences and are happy to identify themselves by class.
- Postmodernists conveniently ignore the fact that consumption depends on jobs and levels of income. Poverty can inhibit any desire to pursue a postmodern lifestyle.
- The evidence regarding class differences in areas such as education and health overwhelmingly indicates the continuing importance of social class.

Key concepts

underclass; welfare dependency; New Right; postmodernism; consumption; choice

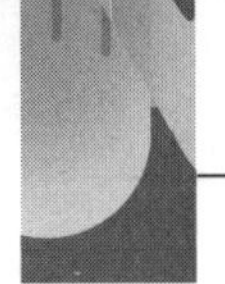

Theories of stratification and class inequality

Functionalism

Functionalists argue that stratification and inequality perform a positive function for society. For example, Davis and Moore say that stratification makes a contribution to social order — therefore, class inequality is beneficial and necessary. The functionalist theory of class stresses the following:

- All societies have to ensure that their most functionally important and senior positions are filled by people who are talented and efficient.
- Talent and skill are in short supply and top jobs require an intensive amount of training and time to acquire the necessary expertise.
- Class societies are essentially meritocracies — high rewards in the form of income and status motivate gifted people to make the necessary sacrifices in terms of education and training.
- Members of society generally agree (i.e. value consensus) that stratification is necessary because education socialises them into accepting meritocratic principles. Consequently most members of society accept whatever social position they achieve.
- Qualifications and therefore the stratification system function to allocate all individuals to an occupational role that suits their abilities (role allocation).
- Class position is therefore a fair reflection of people's talents.
- Stratification encourages all members of society to work to the best of their ability. For example, those at the top wish to retain their advantages, while those below wish to improve their position.

Evaluation

- There is little consensus about rewards. There is substantial resentment about the unequal distribution of income as illustrated by the controversy over pay for top businessmen, bankers and celebrities.
- Davis and Moore suggest that unequal rewards are the product of consensus, but they may be the result of some groups being able to use economic and political power to increase their rewards against the will of others.
- High rewards also go to people who play no functionally important role but simply live off the interest on their wealth.
- Many occupations can be seen to be functionally essential to the smooth running of society but are not highly rewarded, e.g. nursing, while some celebrities who make no discernible contribution earn millions.
- Davis and Moore neglect the dysfunctions of stratification, e.g. that poverty is a major problem for people and negatively impacts on mortality, health, education and family life.

Key concepts

functional; meritocracy; value consensus; role allocation; dysfunction

Marxism

Marxists see all history as the history of class struggle. Apart from a primitive form of communism which existed in early hunting and gathering societies, all stages of history have been characterised by class-based societies. The Marxist theory of class stresses the following:

- Social class is essentially the product of the mode of production of a society.
- The mode of production of capitalist societies is industrial, whereas in feudal societies it was agricultural.
- The mode of production is made up of the relationship between the means of production and the social relations of production.
- The means of production refers to resources such as land, factories, machinery and raw materials, which are owned by the capitalist class or bourgeoisie.
- The workers or proletariat do not own productive property and their only asset is their labour power.
- The social relations of production refers to the economic relationship between the bourgeoisie and proletariat, as the latter hires out its labour to the former.
- The relationship between the bourgeoisie and proletariat is deeply unequal, exploitative and creates class conflict.
- Inequality, exploitation and conflict result from the fact that it is in the interests of the capitalist class to keep wages low in order to increase profits.
- Capitalism's relentless pursuit of profit means that workers lose control over the work process as new technology is introduced, thus creating the potential for alienation.
- However, workers rarely think that they are being exploited because they are suffering from false class consciousness — they have been fooled by ideological apparatuses such as education and the media into believing that capitalism is fair and natural.

Neo-Marxism

Neo-Marxists have tended to focus on the relationship between:

- the infrastructure, i.e. the capitalist economy and particularly the social relationships of production characterised by class inequality, exploitation and subordination, and
- the superstructure, i.e. all the major social institutions of society, e.g. education, the mass media, religion, the law, the political system.

Neo-Marxists argue that the function of the superstructure is the reproduction and legitimation of class inequality through the transmission of ruling class ideology. Moreover, the superstructure operates through the education system and the media to encourage the poor and the powerless to passively accept class stratification.

Althusser describes the educational system as an ideological state apparatus and argues that the idea that educational systems are meritocratic, i.e. that ability is the major mechanism of success, is a myth. Those born into ruling or middle-class backgrounds are more likely to achieve because of the way schools' hidden curriculum

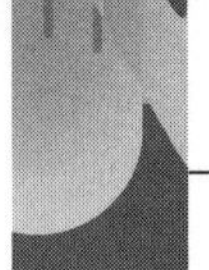

is organised, i.e. their cultural values and outlook are rewarded with access to universities and qualifications.

Bourdieu suggests that the children of the upper and middle class are ensured educational and economic success because they have cultural capital (i.e. the values and attitudes that teachers value) and economic advantages, e.g. their parents can afford private education. Working class children, on the other hand, lack cultural capital and are condemned to a life of manual work, most of them leaving education at 16. However, they rarely blame the capitalist system for their 'failure' because the ideology of meritocracy ensures that they blame themselves. The organisation of capitalism therefore is rarely challenged and class inequality is reproduced generation after generation.

The Frankfurt School of Marxists focused on the role of the media in creating a popular culture for the masses that diverted working-class attention away from the organisation of capitalism and towards consumerism, celebrity culture and trivia. Marcuse argues that capitalism has been very successful in encouraging the working class to focus on acquiring 'false needs', i.e. the latest consumer goods, and diverting their attention away from inequality.

Neo-Marxists argue that television soap operas and celebrity news are the focus of the popular media. Little attention is paid by the media to political and economic life. The media rarely look critically at the way capitalism is organised. Moreover, people are encouraged to compete with each other for material success and consumer goods. Class inequality is rarely challenged.

Evaluation

- Marxism is an economic determinist or reductionist theory in that all major ideas are seen to be the product of the economic relationship between the bourgeoisie and proletariat. However, conflicts around nationalism, ethnicity and gender cannot be explained adequately in economic terms.
- Marx made certain predictions, for example that the working class would experience poverty and misery, the middle class would disappear, and that communism would replace capitalism, which have not come true.
- Saunders (1990) argues that neo-Marxism smacks of arrogance because it claims to know a 'truth' that is hidden from everybody else.
- Marxist theory dismisses the perspective of working-class people as the product of false class consciousness. Working-class people are dismissed as cultural dopes.
- Western class-based capitalist societies may have problems such as poverty and homelessness, but they have a good record in terms of democracy and trade union rights. The working class therefore may be sensibly reconciled to capitalism, rather than falsely conscious.

Key concepts

class struggle; mode of production; means of production; social relations of production; bourgeoisie; proletariat; labour power; exploitation; class conflict; surplus value; alienation; false class consciousness; ideological apparatus; hidden curriculum; false needs

Max Weber

Weber was critical of Marx for neglecting the sources of power that did not arise primarily out of economic relationships. The Weberian theory of class includes the following points:

- Weber saw class and status as two separate but related sources of power, which have separate but related effects on people's life chances.
- Weber defined class in terms of market position, e.g. income, skills and qualifications, rather than purely ownership of productive property so, for example, within the working class skilled workers may be better off than unskilled workers.
- Status inequality can derive from class inequality. People who occupy high occupational roles generally have high social status, but this can also derive from other sources of power such as their gender, race, religion etc.
- Weber noted that some status was also linked to how people spend their money, some people deriving status from conspicuous consumption, such as buying expensive designer products.

Evaluation

- Marxists argue that Weber was too wrapped up in identifying trivial market details, and neglected the basic split between capitalists and workers.
- Marxists argue that class and status are strongly linked — the capitalist class not only has wealth but also high status and political power. Weber recognised that these overlap but suggested that a person can have wealth but little status, e.g. a lottery winner.
- Marxists argue that gender and ethnic differences are essentially rooted in class differences, but Weber saw them as being separate and distinct.

Postmodernism

Postmodernists reject the grand narratives of the stratification theories of functionalism, Marxism and Weberianism.

They argue that capitalist societies have undergone major changes in the past 30 years — modern industrial society, which was focused on producing manufactured goods, has evolved into a post-industrial society based on the production of knowledge, where the service sector of the economy is now more important in terms of employment than the primary and secondary sectors.

The collective social identity of modern industrial societies was mainly based upon social class. However, postmodernists argue that media-saturated postmodern societies are characterised by diversity, plurality and consumption. Subjective individual identity is now more important than objective collective identity.

Postmodernists such as Waters argue that social class is in terminal decline as a source of identity and that consumption is now the central driving force in terms of how people organise their daily lives.

Postmodernists argue that people now use a variety of influences, e.g. globalisation, multiculturalism and media to construct personal identity.

Postmodern stratification is therefore about lifestyle choices, fragmented association (people never belong to or identify with one group for very long), being seduced into conspicuous consumption by advertising and constant changes in people's identities as they pick and mix from the rich variety of influences.

Evaluation

- Critics of postmodernism believe that postmodernists exaggerate the degree of social change, e.g. manufacturing industry is still very important.
- Surveys suggest that the traditional sources of collective identity, i.e. class, gender and ethnicity, are still centrally important to people's sense of identity.

Key concepts

status; consumption; conspicuous consumption; market position

Gender inequality

During the past 30 years, the number of female workers in the UK has risen by 2.45 million whereas the number of male workers has risen by only 0.5 million.

There was a similar number of men and women in work in 2008 — 13.6 million of each sex — compared with 1985, when men filled 2 million more jobs than women.

The UK labour market is characterised by horizontal segregation, meaning that different sectors of employment are dominated by either male or female workers — primary school teaching is overwhelmingly female, whereas higher education has only about 25% of jobs filled by women.

- In the public sector, women are mainly employed in health and social work and education, where they made up 79% and 73% of the workforce respectively in 2006. In the private sector, women are over-concentrated in clerical, administrative, retail and personal services, such as catering, whereas men are mainly found in the skilled manual and upper professional sectors (EOC 2006).
- According to the Office of National Statistics (ONS) in 2008 men and women were still likely to follow very different career paths. Men were ten times more likely than women to be employed in skilled trades (19% compared with 2%) and are also more likely to be managers and senior officials. A fifth of women in employment do administrative or secretarial work compared with 4% of men. Women are also more likely than men to be employed in the personal services and in sales and customer services. Men are more likely to be self-employed than women. Nearly three-quarters of the 3.8 million self-employed people in 2008 were men, a proportion that has remained the same since early 1997.

The UK labour market is also characterised by vertical segregation, meaning that males and females dominate different levels of jobs in terms of status, skill and pay.

- The evidence suggests that within occupational groups, women tend to be concentrated at the lower levels. When women do gain access to the upper professional or management sector, the evidence suggests that they encounter a 'glass ceiling' — a situation in which promotion appears to be possible, but restrictions or discrimination create barriers that prevent it. For example, 66% of full-time secondary school teachers in 2007 in England were female but only 30% of secondary school heads were. In 2007 male primary school teachers were three times more likely than females to become head teachers.
- In 2008, women made up only 11% of directors of the top 100 British companies, a quarter of NHS consultants,10% of high court judges and just two out of 17 national newspaper editors.
- The Equality and Human Rights Commission noted in 2008 that women lack access to the most powerful jobs and that it will take 55 years at the current rate of progress for women to achieve equal status with men at senior levels in the judiciary and 73 years for equality to be achieved in top management jobs in Britain's top 100 companies.

A gender pay gap exists. The EOC estimated in 2007 that the average pay gap between men and women has remained steady at 17%.

- Hourly pay statistics are only one aspect of the inequality women experience in pay. If specific occupations are examined, the gap is much greater than 12.6%. It rises to 22.3% in the private sector although it is only 13.4% in the state sector. For example, the difference in earnings in 2006 between men and women in health and social work jobs was 32%, and 41% in banking and insurance.
- Even women who have managed to reach top positions are not immune from pay inequality. In 2008, the Chartered Management Institute (CMI) showed that the average female executive is earning £32,614 a year, compared with the average male executive who earns £46,269.
- The income gap is widest in retirement at 47% in 2006. While retired men got nearly half their income from non-state or occupational pensions, retired women got only a quarter of their income from these sources.

Women are more likely than men to be employed in part-time work and in temporary or casual labour.

Male unemployment is higher than female unemployment, although this may be due to the gender bias of official statistics, which do not recognise housewives as available for work.

Evaluation

- There is some evidence that horizontal segregation may be in decline because of the general decline in male employment.
- Recent female trends in educational success may also weaken horizontal segregation of the labour market.
- Vertical segregation in female-dominated careers like nursing may worsen for women with movement of men into these areas.

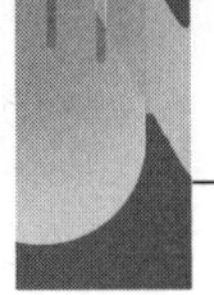

- Hakim argues that the feminisation of the labour force is exaggerated because most of the increase is in part-time rather than full-time work.
- Official female unemployment rates are rising faster than male unemployment rates.

Synoptic evidence of gender inequality

Gender and poverty

Some sociologists claim that inequalities in employment mean there has been a 'feminisation of poverty' because:

- Women generally do not earn as much as men.
- Women are more likely to be in low-status, low-skilled and therefore low-paid jobs, even in the service sector.
- More women than men work part-time.
- More women are excluded from work because they are full-time carers.
- Women may be excluded from sections of the job market because of employer stereotyping and discrimination.
- Women may be denied access to professional and managerial jobs because of the 'glass ceiling'.
- Older women are less likely to have occupational pensions because they may have spent substantial periods of their lives in the home as mothers and housewives. Poverty is common among female pensioners, who tend to outlive their partners.
- 90% of lone parents are female. The lack of free nursery care in the UK means that it is difficult for poorer women to go out to work.

Gender and family

- The idea that equality is a central characteristic of marriage is strongly opposed by feminist sociologists. Studies of professional couples indicate that only a minority genuinely share housework and childcare. Dryden's (1999) qualitative study of 17 married couples found that women still had major responsibility for housework and childcare.
- The Future Foundation (2000) found that women were receiving more help in the home from husbands and boyfriends than previous generations. Two-thirds of men said they did more around the home than their fathers.
- Evidence from family studies suggest that women are likely to experience a 'dual burden' — they are expected to be mainly responsible for the bulk of domestic tasks despite holding down full-time jobs.

Gender and education

- Feminists have pointed out that, despite the fact that girls' achievements in education outstrip those of males, the 'hidden curriculum' means that subject choices in secondary schools and in further and higher education still tend to be gender-stereotyped.
- This leads to reinforcing gender divisions in the workplace because choice of degree subjects is likely to influence career.

Gender and health

- Graham points out that women have higher rates of illness than men, especially mental illness.

- Bernard suggests that marriage makes women sick because married women experience worse health than married men and single women. Women may experience greater stress than men because they are likely to care for both children and other relatives, i.e. ageing parents.

Theories of gender inequality

Liberal feminism

Liberal feminists argue that gender roles are largely constructed through the socialisation process, primarily in the family, but also through, for example, the education system and the media. Gender role socialisation reproduces a sexual division of labour in which masculinity is seen as dominant and femininity as subordinate.

- Liberal feminist research in the 1970s, in particular, focused on how the dominant images of females stressed marriage as a priority and education and careers as secondary.
- Ann Oakley argues that the main reason for the subordination of women in the labour market is the dominance of the mother–housewife role for women, and that ideas such as the maternal instinct and maternal deprivation serve primarily to ensure men's dominance of the labour market. Oakley found that part-time women workers gave responsibilities to their husband and children as their main reason for not taking up full-time work.
- In the 1990s, liberal feminists suggested that these processes were coming to an end. Both Sue Lees' and Sue Sharpe's work on the attitudes of teenage girls suggest that education and careers are now a priority for young women, with females recently enjoying great educational success. Wilkinson has referred to the radical difference in attitudes of the current generation of women compared with previous generations as a 'genderquake'.
- Liberal feminists suggest that this 'genderquake' has come about because of major changes in the economy, i.e. the movement from primary/secondary means of production to tertiary or service.
- Liberal feminists are very optimistic because they have observed that since the 1970s women have made great progress in terms of acquisition of economic power through careers, improvements in equal opportunities legislation and pay, political power through greater representation in government and social power through contraception and divorce. They believe that patriarchy or male dominance is in decline.

Evaluation

- Sylvia Walby (1990) suggests that although there is evidence that masculinity and femininity are socially constructed, it does not explain why men are usually in positions of dominance and women subordinate.
- Liberal feminism implies that people passively accept their gender identities — it underestimates the degree of resistance by some women and consequently the range of female identities that are available to women today.
- Liberal feminism fails to acknowledge that women's experiences differ according to social class and race.

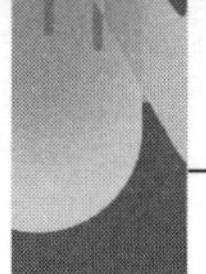

– Some liberal feminists advise caution in our interpretation of educational and occupational trends. Women are still located in educational and job ghettoes, and many commentators have observed that representations of women in the mass media are still very sexist.

Key concepts

liberal feminism; gender role socialisation; sexual division of labour; subordination; feminisation of labour force; horizontal segregation; vertical segregation; glass ceiling; gender pay gap

Dual labour market theory

The 'dual labour market' theory of Barron and Norris, which focuses on gender inequalities in employment, is very influenced by Max Weber's ideas about status. They argue that there exist two markets for labour — the primary sector characterised by secure, well-paid and high status jobs, which are dominated by men, and the secondary sector, characterised by insecure, low-paid, low-status unskilled jobs. Barron and Norris point out that women are more likely to be found in the secondary sector. They are less likely to gain primary-sector employment because:

- Employers have stereotypical beliefs about the unsuitability of women workers, e.g. employers may believe that women's careers are likely to be interrupted by producing and rearing children, and consequently may not be willing invest in training for them.
- Promotion is often dependent on continuous service, which matches the life experiences of men better than women.
- Caplow argues that the husband's career may dictate the geographical movement of the family, and consequently undermine the continuity in women's careers.
- The legal and political framework supporting women is weak, e.g. both the Equal Pay Act and Sex Discrimination Act fail to protect women's employment rights adequately.
- The social organisation of work in Western societies is essentially patriarchal, which makes discrimination against women 'natural'.

This theory undermines the liberal feminist assumption that better qualifications and changes in women's ambitions will automatically dismantle gender divisions in employment.

Evaluation

– Bradley points out that the theory fails to explain inequalities within the same sector. For example, teaching is not a secondary labour market, yet women are less likely than men to gain high status jobs in this profession.

Key concepts

dual labour market; primary/secondary sectors; patriarchy

Marxist feminism

Marxist feminists suggest that capitalism exploits both male and female workers, but as women are more likely to work part-time rather than full-time, they are more likely to be part of a 'reserve army of labour' hired by the capitalist class when the economy is prospering but laid off when recession sets in. Marxists argue that women constitute a more disposable part of the workforce because:

- Women change jobs more frequently than men so they are more vulnerable in recession, the last people recruited usually being the first to be made redundant.
- Traditionally, women were generally less skilled and relatively under-unionised compared with male workers. They are also more likely than men to be employed part-time. Consequently, it is easier for employers to sack them.
- Capitalist ideologies locate women in the home, the common belief being that married women have less right to a job than men. When women are made unemployed, such ideology suggests that 'women have gone back to their proper jobs'.

Evaluation

- The 'reserve army of labour' theory has been criticised because it fails to explain why jobs are gendered, i.e. why there are men's jobs and women's jobs.
- The theory fails to explain why women occupy the housewife role.
- Moreover, if women are cheaper than men, surely capitalists would get rid of the more expensive men first.

Key concepts

reserve army of labour; capitalism; ideology

Triple-systems theory

Sylvia Walby's 'triple systems theory' develops the concept of patriarchy to explain gender stratification. She suggests that patriarchy has three elements to it:

(1) Subordination — patriarchal institutions like the family, media and education inevitably produce unequal relations between men and women via gender role socialisation.

(2) Oppression — women experience sexism because patriarchal ideology results in men discriminating against them on the basis of unfounded stereotypes.

(3) Exploitation — men exploit women's skills and labour without rewarding them sufficiently, e.g. in the home.

Walby argues that patriarchy is not only about the interaction of men and women in these three respects, but that it also intersects with capitalism and racism to produce gender stratification. Such inequality can be seen in six social structures:

(1) The patriarchal mode of production, which exploits female domestic labour within the family.

(2) The fact of patriarchal relations in paid work is reflected in vertical and horizontal segregation at work.

(3) Patriarchal relations in the state — the state acts in the interests of men rather than women, e.g. in terms of taxation, welfare rules and the weakness of laws protecting women at work.

(4) Acts of male violence against women, such as rape and domestic violence, persist as major social problems.

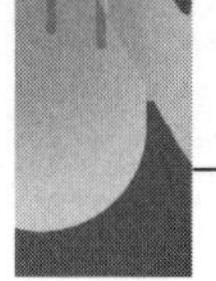

(5) A sexual double standard exists, which endorses multiple sexual partners for men but condemns the same behaviour in women.

(6) Agencies like the mass media represent women in narrow social roles, e.g. as sex objects and mother–housewives.

Catherine Hakim and rational choice theory

Catherine Hakim is extremely critical of all the previous feminist positions. She argues that feminist theories of patriarchy are both inaccurate and misleading, and that women are not victims of unfair employment practices. According to Hakim:

- Women with children make rational choices about their futures — they believe that childcare is just as important a career as employment.
- The lack of women in top jobs and their domination of part-time work does not reflect a lack of free childcare, employer discrimination or weak laws but reflects the rational choice to put children and family first.

Evaluation

– Ginn and Arber point out that all too often it is employer attitudes rather than women's attitudes that confine women to the secondary labour market.

Key concepts

rational choice; subordination; oppression; discrimination; exploitation; patriarchy

Ethnic inequality

Ethnic-minority men are over-represented in the service sector. The distribution industry (including restaurants and retail businesses) is the largest single source of service-sector jobs for men from ethnic-minority groups, employing 70% of Bangladeshi and 58% of Chinese men compared with only 17% of whites. One in eight taxi drivers in the UK come from Pakistani backgrounds.

- Very few ethnic minorities are engaged in white collar, professional or managerial work although people from Indian and Chinese backgrounds are more likely than other ethnic minority groups to be found in middle-class non-manual occupations such as accountancy, law and medicine. For example, approximately one in 20 working Indian men is a medical practitioner — almost ten times the national average.
- Ethnic minority men were less likely than white men in 2004 to be employed in skilled trades (11.7% compared with 20.2%) and more likely than white men to be employed in unskilled 'elementary occupations' (15.2% compared with 11.5%).

Ethnic minorities generally earn lower incomes than white people, and they are more likely to work in the types of employment in which wages are generally low.

- Research by the Joseph Rowntree Foundation in 2007 found that men from ethnic minorities in managerial and professional jobs earn up to 25% less than their white colleagues. Black African and Bangladeshi men were most likely to face the greatest pay discrimination. Indian men were the least likely to be discriminated against but they were still earning less than white men doing the same job.

In 2004 whites had the lowest unemployment rates at 5%. The highest unemployment rates were among black Caribbean men (14%) and men from black African, mixed and Bangladeshi groups (each 13%). Unemployment rates were slightly lower for Pakistani and Chinese men (11% and 10% respectively). Indian men had the lowest unemployment rates among the ethnic minority groups at 7%. 37% of Bangladeshis and 35% of Pakistanis aged between 16 and 24 were unemployed compared with 11% of white young people.

An African-Caribbean graduate is twice as likely to be unemployed than a white graduate. African men with degrees are seven times more likely to be unemployed than white male graduates.

Research by the Joseph Rowntree Foundation in 2007 showed that 40% of ethnic minority communities in the UK live in poverty — double the poverty rates of white communities. Half of all ethnic minority children in the UK live in poverty.

Racial discrimination and institutional racism across a range of organisations is recognised as a major contributor to unemployment, low wages and poverty among ethnic minority groups. For example, one in eight members of ethnic minority groups have reported discrimination at job interviews. Bradley (2007) reports that almost one-third (31%) of black Caribbean women had seen less experienced or less qualified people promoted above them, and a third had experienced racist comments at work.

Bradley (2007) revealed that 54% of black Caribbean women often had difficulty finding work (compared with only 34% of white women), and are often forced to take jobs below their skills and experience levels.

Pakistani and Bangladeshi women have low economic activity rates, high unemployment rates and are more heavily concentrated than white women in a restricted range of occupations (including retail, clerical work and educational support work).

Synoptic evidence of ethnic inequality

Poverty and ethnic minorities

- Ethnic minority groups are more likely than whites to experience poverty. Two-thirds of Pakistani and Bangladeshi people, nearly 50% of African-origin people and a third of African-Caribbean origin people are estimated to be poor.
- Alcock identifies a range of different forms of poverty and exclusion that ethnic minorities in the UK experience, including poor access to good quality private housing and health and welfare benefits, educational inequalities, lack of political representation, being the victims of negative media stereotyping and over-zealous policing, and fear from racist attacks.
- Many aspects of social exclusion experienced by ethnic minorities reinforce each other. Poor, damp housing can lead to poor health in children, time off school and,

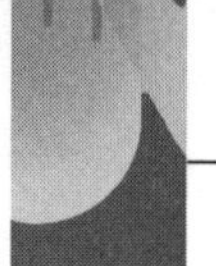

in the long term, few qualifications. This in turn leads to low-skilled and low-paid jobs or unemployment.

Health and ethnic minorities

- Infant mortality is 100% higher among the children of African-Caribbean or Pakistani mothers than among children of white mothers.
- Pakistani and Bangladeshi people are five times more likely to be diagnosed with diabetes and 50% more likely to have coronary heart disease than white people.

Education and ethnic minorities

- Bangladeshi, Pakistani and black pupils achieve less than other pupils at all stages of compulsory education. In 2003, only 41% of Pakistani pupils, 37% of black pupils, and 45% of Bangladeshi pupils achieved five or more GCSEs at grades A* to C, compared with 51% of white pupils and 65% of Indian pupils.
- African-Caribbean pupils are three times more likely to be permanently excluded from school than white pupils.
- Over half of children from Asian households are eligible for free school meals. Children who were eligible for free school meals were far less likely to achieve expected outcomes for Key Stages 1–4.

Housing and ethnic minorities

- 70% of all people from ethnic minorities live in the 88 most deprived local authority districts compared with 40% of the general population.
- Ethnic minority groups are more likely to live in poor quality and overcrowded housing.

Crime and ethnic minorities

- Racial harassment incidents are widespread and under-reported — only 5% of incidents are reported to the police.
- African-Caribbean youth are eight times more likely to be stopped and searched by the police than white people.
- African-Caribbean people are over-represented in the prison population. They are nine times more likely to be in prison than their white counterparts.
- Asians are 50 times and African-Caribbeans are 36 times more likely to be victims of a racially motivated attack.

Theories of ethnic inequalities

Weberian explanations

Parkin argues that modern societies are characterised by class and ethnic inequality, with status and power in the hands of the majority ethnic group. Racism and prejudice makes it difficult for ethnic minority groups to compete equally for jobs, housing etc.

Racism refers to the combination of discriminatory practices, unequal power relations and negative attitudes practised by majority ethnic groups against minorities.

Prejudice refers to negative and stereotypical attitudes towards ethnic minorities held by some sections of a majority population. These prejudices are usually factually incorrect, exaggerated and distorted.

Discrimination is defined as that prejudice which is actually put into practice in regard to jobs, housing, racial attacks and policing.

Institutional racism is the idea that racist assumptions are built into the rules and routines of Britain's social institutions. This type of racism has become so habitual and institutionalised that it is not recognised as racism.

Ethnic minority manual workers are technically part of the working class, but are likely to face racism in the form of prejudice and discrimination from the white working class, so that they suffer from status inequality in addition to class inequality.

Even middle-class Asians doing professional jobs may experience prejudicial attitudes from both the white middle and working classes.

The dual labour market theory

The Weberian dual labour market theory of Barron and Norris argues that the primary sector (secure, well-paid jobs) is dominated by white men, and the secondary sector (low-paid, unskilled and insecure jobs) are dominated by women and black people.

- Ethnic minorities are less likely to gain primary-sector employment because employers have racist beliefs about their unsuitability, and even practise discrimination against them either when they apply for jobs or by denying them responsibility and promotion.
- The legal and political framework supporting black people is weak. The Race Relations Act, which is supposed to protect them from discriminatory practices, is generally thought to be feeble. Trade unions are generally white-dominated and tend to favour white workers.
- Some Weberians, especially Rex and Tomlinson, argue that ethnic minority experience of both class and status inequality and racism leads to poverty. A black underclass may exist which is marginalised, alienated and frustrated, and which sometimes erupts in the form of inner-city riots if young blacks feel, for example, that they are being harassed by the police.

Evaluation

– Commentators such as Murray and Marsland blame the culture of some ethnic minorities for their poverty and unemployment, claiming that young African-Caribbeans, in particular, are workshy and welfare-dependent. However, surveys indicate their norms and values with regard to work are no different from mainstream society.

– The existence of a black underclass has not been proved — there is considerable overlap between white and black populations in terms of poverty and unemployment.

+ However, the concept of status inequality may help to explain some apparent divisions between the white and black working class, in terms of unemployment and promotion into white-collar work.

Key concepts

racism; discrimination; prejudice; institutional racism; dual labour market; status inequality

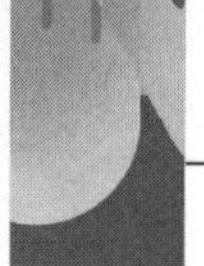

Marxist explanations

Marxists are adamant that black people are part of the exploited working class and that status inequality is less important than class inequality. However, they do acknowledge that racism is a powerful influence in modern society and suggest that it is used as an ideological weapon to attain three objectives:

(1) Racism means that black unemployment, low pay and poor conditions in the workplace do not generate controversy, ensuring that employers can treat black people as a reserve army of labour, to be hired when the economy expands and laid off when recession sets in.

(2) White workers are encouraged to perceive black workers as a threat to their jobs, so that employers can use the threat of cheaper black workers to control their workforce — especially if there are hints that white workers are planning to strike for higher pay. This tactic 'divides and rules' the black and white working class.

(3) Social problems caused by the mismanagement of capitalism can also be blamed on ethnic minorities. Black people can be scapegoated for unemployment (through beliefs such as 'they've come over here to take our jobs') or inner-city decline ('this was a nice neighbourhood before they moved in').

Evaluation

- It is difficult to prove that racism is a capitalist ideology — it may benefit capitalism in the long term but this is not evidence that it functions exclusively as an ideological apparatus.
- Marxists tend to talk about racism as if the capitalist class had deliberately constructed it to control both black and white workers. However, there is no evidence that the capitalist class is responsible for its existence or its maintenance.

Neo-Marxist explanations

The neo-Marxist Miles argues that we should see ethnic minorities as members of 'racialised class fractions', meaning that although ethnic minorities are part of the working class, there are significant cultural differences between them and the white working class which result in them stressing aspects of their ethnic identity. Young African-Caribbeans, for example, may stress black power through membership of the Rastafarian sect or elements of black history, whilst Asians may stress family ties and community.

- Miles also notes that some ethnic minorities who are members of the middle class may see their interests lying with capitalism. The Asian emphasis on entrepreneurship, enterprise and mutual support may be advantageous in achieving business success.
- There is evidence that increasing numbers of ethnic minorities are entering the ranks of the professional middle class, although often the lower-middle class, where status and pay are not high, or in lower and middle management rather than top management positions.
- Miles points out that racism probably means that the white middle class will never accept that Asian professionals have the same status as they have, and may engage in 'white flight' from areas successful Asians are moving into.

Key concepts

class inequality; reserve army of labour; divide and rule; racism as ideology; moral panic; scapegoating; racialised class fractions; white flight

Age inequality

Age intersects with other structural influences such as class, gender and ethnicity and result in inequalities experienced by both the elderly and the young.

The elderly

Bradley (1996) refers to age as the neglected dimension of inequality. In pre-industrial societies, the elderly have status and influence but in industrial societies, the elderly are seen as lacking the ability to contribute meaningfully and are excluded from full involvement in society.

- Help the Aged (2008) suggests that in 2006, 33% of UK pensioners or 1.2 million people were living in poverty.
- This poverty is having a negative effect on health — one in four of the elderly poor suffered illness as a direct result of poverty.
- It is estimated that by 2010, 1.2 million pensioners will experience 'fuel poverty', whereby spending on electricity, coal and gas takes up a disproportionate share of their income.
- People who are poor in old age are likely to be those who have earned least in their lives, because they are less likely to have access to private pensions. Oppenheim and Harker (1996) found that 73% of male employees receive company pensions compared with 68% of female full-time employees and only 31% of female part-timers.
- Davidson notes that women receive lower occupational pensions because they are likely to have their careers interrupted because of pregnancy and childcare.
- Mordaunt et al (2003) note that twice as many elderly women than men rely on benefits to supplement their state pensions.
- Davidson notes that ethnic minority elderly people are less likely to have access to private occupational pensions because they are most likely to have been employed in low-paid manual work or been unemployed.
- Scase and Scase (2000) note that the elderly can be divided into two economic groups: affluent middle-class ex-professionals, and those on or close to the breadline who are forced to work beyond retirement age to avoid severe poverty.
- Ray et al. (2006) notes that retirement age often differs according to social class, i.e. many political and business leaders are able to resist the 'official' retirement requirement and continue earning well into old age.

Ageism

The elderly may be exposed to ageism — a process of negative stereotyping and discrimination on the basis of age. The young can also be victims of ageism, although it probably affects the quality of life of the elderly more than that of the young. Ageism takes several forms:

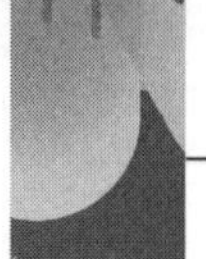

- Greengross argues that ageism has become institutionalised, e.g. age barriers set by the state mean that the elderly cannot participate in many civic duties such as jury service.
- In the NHS older people may be subject to discrimination by being denied particular treatments or operations because of their age.
- Ray et al. note that the elderly are often excluded from work because employers assume lower competence than younger workers.
- Discrimination by financial services companies may mean that older people have difficulty getting insurance, a credit card or a loan.
- The mass media represent youth as beautiful and old age as the greatest threat to well-being. Carrigan and Szmigin (2000) argue that the advertising industry either ignores older people or presents them in the form of negative stereotypes.
- Ageist stereotypes are important because they are often the only experience that the young have of the elderly.
- Ageist stereotypes create perceptions of old age as a time of dependency, poor health and poverty despite the fact this is not the experience of all the elderly.
- Ray et al. claim that the elderly are often infantilised, ignored and treated in a patronising and disrespectful fashion.

The young

The young also make up a large sub-group of the poor:

- The government has estimated that 5 million children in the UK live in poverty.
- Many young people of working age face social deprivation caused by low pay, student loans, and in some case ineligibility for benefits.
- In 2001 the unemployment rate for those under 25 was over 20%. However, some groups of young people face greater inequality because of their gender or ethnicity.
- The ending of student grants now means that more young people are dependent upon their parents for a greater length of time.
- Low pay and employment mean that it is virtually impossible for some young people to get on the property ladder.
- The number of young homeless has increased.
- Campbell suggests that some young women use having a baby as a means of acquiring adult status in a society which has increasingly closed down other options for them.
- Young men who live in severely deprived areas with little prospect of work may turn to crime such as car theft and drugs in order to obtain both material success and status.
- Most young workers earn relatively little, e.g. 235,000 18- to 20-year-old workers earn the minimum wage. More than two-thirds of McDonalds' staff are aged under 20.

- Nearly 2 million young people aged between 16 and 24 in full-time education are also in paid employment. Two-thirds of Pizza Hut's 'crew' staff are in full-time education, as are one-fifth of Sainsbury's store staff.

Theories of age inequality

Functionalist explanations

Functionalists consider age to be more important compared with pre-industrial society in which family was the most important determinant of a person's status.

- Parsons claimed that industrial societies provide role sets that create a link between the family and wider society.
- Belonging to a particular age group is important because it helps integrate people into society. People evolve from one age group to another. Some functionalists see the elderly as disengaging with society in order to make room for the young — thus maintaining social cohesion.

Weberian explanations

Weberians argue that each age cohort can be considered as an age stratum, i.e. with its own market position and relative status. They do not explain, however, why older groups tend to have a worse market position and status relative to other groups.

Marxist explanations

Marxists have suggested that the elderly are ignored because they are economically unattractive as consumers: they don't have the disposable income that younger people do. They consequently have little status and power.

Marxists argue that in capitalist societies work is the central source of status, so retirement means that the elderly are deprived of a major source of respect, identity, friendship and economic security. Those in work can perceive them as a burden because they see themselves as paying for the economic upkeep of the elderly.

Marxists see the young as providing a cheap pool of flexible labour for capitalism. Young people do not have dependants and consequently are willing to work for low wages. In terms of full-time employment, their lack of experience legitimates low pay, and competition for jobs keeps wages low.

Postmodernist explanations

Postmodernists point out that increased life expectancy coupled with a planned retirement has given some old people the ability to become conspicuous consumers.

Postmodernists are interested in how popular culture defines identity. They argue that age is increasingly tied into consumerism. A growing number of middle-class, elderly consumers may well undermine the view that the elderly lack status and power.

Research methods

Exploring sociological research: essential concepts

Reliability

This concept relates mainly to the process of carrying out sociological research, and is concerned with the way in which data are gathered, focusing on whether the evidence is collected scientifically.

Some sociologists argue that 'replication' is an important characteristic of scientific method, i.e. if another sociologist is able to repeat (or replicate) findings, using the same method and a comparable sample, reliability is said to be high.

Validity

This concept refers to the degree to which the research activity actually measures what it sets out to measure.

- To ensure validity, it is important to select a method that will reflect the reality of who or what is being explored.
- How the research is designed in terms of those selected to take part and the operationalisation of the hypothesis are central to bringing about validity.
- Primary research, i.e. that carried out by sociologists themselves, usually turns out to have more validity than secondary research, i.e. official statistics or documents produced by other agencies such as the state.

Representativeness

This concept focuses on the sampling process, i.e. how those who take part in the research are chosen. Usually, researchers want to obtain a 'representative' research group, meaning that those taking part in the research have the same social features as the larger group or society to which they belong. For example, if sixth form college students in the UK are being researched, a representative sample should resemble the general population in characteristics such as gender, age, ethnicity, qualifications being studied etc. The sample of sixth form college students used should be representative of sixth form college students in general.

Generalisability

The concept of generalisability has strong links with the concept of representativeness because it refers to researchers taking their findings from the sample and making the assumption that these can be applied to the whole society or the larger social group to which the sample belongs. The aim is to say that what is true of the sample of, say sixth form college students, is highly likely to be true of all sixth form college students.

Primary data

Primary data are gathered 'first-hand' by the sociologist using a variety of methods such as questionnaires or interviews or by observing people's behaviour.

Secondary data

Secondary data are data that have been collected by people who are not sociologists, and published or written down. For example, crime statistics are collected by the police and the courts and collated and published by civil servants at the Home Office every 3 months. Journalists may research crime and publish their findings in the form of a newspaper or magazine article.

Quantitative data

This refers to statistical evidence that is normally collected using primary methods such as questionnaires and structured interviews. It is usually presented in the form of graphs, tables, bar-charts etc. Some sociologists use secondary sources in order to gather statistical evidence. For example, with regard to inequality, official statistics relating to wealth and income collected by the government are useful in determining whether inequality has increased or narrowed over the past 50 years.

Qualitative data

This refers to data that take a written form and provide a more personal account of the social world, e.g. transcripts or summaries of interviews, selected quotations from conversations or descriptions of a place, a group or a situation or a diary entry. This type of data tends to be concerned with how people see or interpret the world around them — it allows respondents to speak for themselves.

Methodological issues and concerns

Good empirical sociologists choose whatever methods work best and this may involve a combination of methods traditionally associated with either the positivist or the interpretivist position.

Positivism

Just as natural scientists (such as biologists, physicists or chemists) believe that behaviour in the natural world is the product of natural laws, positivist sociologists believe that human behaviour is the product of 'social laws' which arise out of the way societies are socially organised. Positivist thinkers believe that sociology is a science

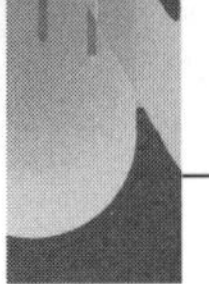

and should adopt four principles that underpin the logic and methods of natural sciences:

(1) Research should be carried out under controlled conditions, as are experiments in laboratories. However, sociologists rarely use laboratory experiments but achieve control through sampling and skilfully-designed questionnaires and interview schedules.

(2) Value freedom and objectivity are essential to positivist research. This means that the sociologist should carry out research and interpret evidence with an open mind, setting aside personal values, political beliefs and prejudices. Positivists believe that subjectivity, i.e. personal views and values, is likely to distort the research and result in unreliable findings.

(3) Reliability is central to positivist research design. Positivists believe that the research should be designed in such a way that other sociologists should be able to inspect the research device, replicate it and obtain similar results in order to verify the evidence gathered.

(4) The research method should be designed so that it generates mainly quantitative data, i.e. statistics that can be converted into tabular or graphical information. Such data have comparative value because they can be observed for patterns, trends etc. and for cause and effect relationships in order to establish 'social facts' about human behaviour.

Positivist methodology in sociological research has tended to focus on the use of quantitative methods, such as social surveys. Positivists have also used experiments, the comparative method, official statistics and content analysis of media reports. Such methods tend to be used by macro-sociology, i.e. research that investigates large-scale social processes, structures and institutions such as how inequalities and differences in employment, income, education etc. may be underpinned by social class, gender, ethnicity and age.

Key concepts

reliability; validity; representativeness; generalisability; positivism; social laws; science; objectivity; value freedom; subjectivity; quantitative; macro-sociology

Interpretivism

Interpretivism (also referred to as anti-positivism, action theory or phenomenology), rejects the positivist idea that social laws shape or determine human behaviour. Interpretivist sociologists suggest that society is the product of individuals interacting with each other in social groups. They argue that sociological research should focus on the shared meanings or interpretations that people use to make sense of their social world. People know how to behave in most situations, e.g. at a funeral, because they have learned these shared meanings.

Interpretivist sociologists stress the following when choosing a research method:

- It is important to appreciate how the world looks from the point of view of those being studied, to see how they interpret the world. This is a form of empathy called *verstehen*.

- Interpretivists emphasise validity rather than reliability. They believe that unique and trusting relationships should be established with those being studied so that a true picture of their lives can be constructed, even though such relationships are often difficult to replicate.
- Ethnography is an important aspect of interpretivist research — interpretivists believe a lot of sociological research is artificial. Filling in questionnaires or being interviewed is not a normal or natural part of people's daily lives. Ethnographic research involves researching the everyday lives of research subjects with minimum interference.
- Reflexivity is an important part of the research process, and refers to the process by which sociologists periodically review the degree of objectivity they have achieved in a research project, their rapport with the respondents and the way they process data, in order to ensure methodological integrity. The researcher should always be aware of how their presence influences the behaviour of the research subjects — known as researcher imposition. The researcher should also be flexible enough to change the content or direction of the research if they are negatively impacting on the data being collected.
- Interpretivists often engage in respondent validation in order to avoid the possibility of researcher imposition. This means that they will build safeguards into their research which involve asking those who take part whether the researchers' interpretation of their behaviour is a valid reflection of what was actually going on at the time.
- Interpretivists argue that cause and effect relationships are impossible to establish in regard to human behaviour because human behaviour is generally unpredictable.

Interpretivist methodology tends towards the use of qualitative methods such as unstructured interviews and observation. Interpretivist sociologists have also used methods such as the examination of historical and personal documents as well as analysis of media reports. These tend to be used by micro-sociology, i.e. research that investigates how people make sense of their daily lives, e.g. how they might subjectively interpret their social class position.

Mixing theoretical approaches

Researchers often use both quantitative/positivist and qualitative/interpretivist methods together in the same research. For example, Phizacklea and Wolkowitz (*Homeworking Women* 1995) use both a national survey for reliability and in-depth interviewing for validity.

Key concepts

interpretivism; social action theory; anti-positivism; phenomenology; shared meanings/interpretations; interaction; qualitative; *verstehen*; reflexivity; researcher imposition; respondent validation; micro-sociology

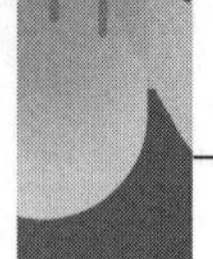

Practical constraints affecting choice of research method

Cost and funding

The cost of the research is a crucial factor in determining the topic of research, the hypothesis and the method to be adopted. A sociologist may not have access to large funds.

- A questionnaire survey only involves printing and postage costs, avoiding the expense of hiring paid interviewers.
- Group or focus interviews might be chosen because they are cheaper than carrying out a series of individual interviews.
- Observation studies are normally carried out over a long period (longitudinal) and are therefore very expensive.
- It is cheaper to use secondary data that have already been collected by agencies such as the state.

Access

Gaining access to a group of people for research purposes can be difficult. Sociologists need to ask themselves whether the research population is:

- accessible
- deviant and therefore potentially threatened by the research
- literate or illiterate
- geographically scattered across the country or concentrated in one place

Difficulty of access to a potential sample of research subjects (respondents) might mean that a preferred method (in-depth interviewing, for example) needs to be changed (perhaps to questionnaires). This is not uncommon, especially if the research issue is a sensitive one, such as finding out the extent of racial prejudice and discrimination practised by white people.

Joining 'exclusive groups' which tend to shut out 'outsiders' or gaining access to them to conduct questionnaires and interviews is not impossible but researchers need to think about both ethics and personal safety. Very often, the sociologist will need to use an intermediary or 'gatekeeper' — a person who has contact with the target population. For example, white researchers may require an Asian or African-Caribbean gatekeeper to access how Asian and black people experience the world of work.

An intermediary plays a key role, since she or he can perhaps vouch for the researcher and help establish a bond of trust between the sociologist and the group in question. Such intermediaries can introduce sociological observers into a group and help reduce the anxieties of other group members who may feel threatened by the newcomer.

Key concepts

longitudinal; focus group interviews; respondents; access; gate-keepers

Sampling

This concept relates to the process by which sociologists select research subjects from a list known as a sampling frame.

- The sampling frame must have the characteristics required for the study in question. For example, it must be a population of people doing manual jobs rather than professionals if the study is looking at how the working class experience their jobs.
- The sampling frame has to be up to date.
- The electoral register is the most common sampling frame used by sociologists but it excludes certain groups, i.e. those aged 17 and under, prisoners, those avoiding paying council tax. Moreover, if it is used months after it is compiled, it will include people who have died or moved away and will not include those who have recently turned 18.
- The Postcode Address File is increasingly popular as a sampling frame.
- Other examples of sampling frames include school registers and doctor's registers. However, permission to use these may only be granted if you can guarantee anonymity, confidentiality and ethical sensitivity, and demonstrate that your research will have positive benefits to the community.
- Deviant or unconventional groups are rarely represented by sampling frames.
- Maps are sometimes used as sampling frames in the absence of lists of particular types of individuals. Sociologists may select areas on a map randomly, and target all households within them.

Random sampling

Random sampling gives everybody in a given population an equal probability of being selected for the sample, minimising the possibility of bias. Certain types of random sampling are most likely to result in representative samples, i.e. those which are most characteristic of the population studied. Representative samples are important because they allow for the possibility of generalising any data collected to the population under scrutiny.

There are various types of random sampling methods:

(1) Simple random sampling involves selecting names from a sampling frame at random. This could be done with a computer. The lottery (Lotto) is a good example of this type of sampling. However, this method does not always guarantee a representative sample.

(2) Systematic random sampling is the most common type of sampling and involves choosing every nth person from a sampling frame. For example, 10 people out of a group of 100 may be chosen by randomly selecting a number between 1 and 10, e.g. 8. Every tenth name after 8 is selected, i.e. the sample consists of numbers 8, 18, 28, 38, 48, 58, 68, 78, 88, 98.

(3) Stratified random sampling is also popular. This type is not concerned with equal probability of selection. Instead, the sociologist requires the sample to mirror the social characteristics of the population in terms of age, social class, gender and ethnicity. The sociologist therefore organises the potential research population into sampling frames that reflect these variables and applies systematic sampling to them. For example, a population of 500 might be divided into 250 men and 250 women and two samples of 25 may be randomly selected from each group.

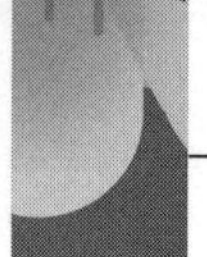

(4) Multi-stage sampling involves selecting a sample from another sample, e.g. in opinion polls before an election, constituencies are chosen and individuals picked at random from these areas.

(5) Cluster sampling occurs when a sampling frame or list is not available. Some sociologists choose clusters of households by selecting areas or streets from a map at random.

Non-random sampling methods

Sampling does not always take a random form. Sometimes sampling frames do not exist for particular groups, especially those labelled deviant or unconventional. The need to get responses from particular types of people may override the scientific objectivity that underpins most random forms of sampling. The most common types of non-random sampling are:

(1) Quota sampling: used when sociologists have a very clear idea of the sample they want and where to find it. For example, a researcher investigating factory workers will probably stand outside a factory because he or she knows that these places will contain a quota of people with the social characteristics he or she is interested in.

(2) Purposive sampling: used when researchers have a clear idea of particular untypical groups that they want to study because they want to test a specific hypothesis. For example, a researcher might wish to study the elderly so he or she purposively target places where he or she will find this group.

(3) Snowball or opportunity sampling: used to sample exceptionally private groups or people who are deviant or criminal and cannot be accessed through conventional means. The technique involves finding and interviewing a person who fits the research needs, and then asking him/her to suggest another person who might be willing to be interviewed. The sample may gradually build up like a snowball. However, snowball sampling may not produce a representative sample.

Key concepts

sampling frame; random sampling; systematic sampling; stratified sampling; multi-stage sampling; cluster sampling; representativeness; generalisability; non-random sampling; snowball sampling; quota sampling; purposive sampling; opportunity sampling

Operationalisation

This refers to transforming a question or hypothesis into something that can be measured through research. It means producing measurable and observable questions for a questionnaire or interview, or categories for an observation or content analysis schedule. There are a number of considerations which influence this process:

- The subject matter of the research will influence the choice of research method. For example, can the subject matter be researched using methods that produce statistical data? Does it demand methods that explore the meaning behind human behaviour? Is the subject matter sensitive or embarrassing?

- The chosen hypothesis needs to be a clear statement, based on careful research and thinking, which makes a causal link between two variables. The hypothesis is either verified or refuted by the research findings.
- The research population often needs to be operationalised in terms of social class, age, gender and ethnicity.
- Social class is often central to a research hypothesis and it is important that sociologists clearly state how a concept is being operationalised, e.g. for many years, both the government and sociologists used job type as the basis for social class (as in the Registrar-General's scale) but since 2000 social class has been operationalised by asking people questions relating to the nature of their employment (Are you an employer or employed? Are you full-time, part-time or temporary? etc.) and their work situation.
- Ethnicity can be difficult to operationalise because the UK is a multicultural society made up of a diversity of ethnic groups. A common term such as 'Asian' may require breaking down into specific cultural and religious groups in order to produce valid data.
- The hypothesis itself needs to be broken down into its measurable components. For example, the hypothesis, 'middle-class professionals have more economic, cultural and social capital than other middle-class groups' needs to break down the three concepts of economic, cultural and social capital into question form so that their influence on the professional middle class and other middle class groups can be measured.

If the researcher is asking questions about attitudes or sensitive subjects such as racism, attitudinal scales may be used, e.g. 'On a scale of 1–5, 1 being "strongly agree" and 5 being "strongly disagree", consider the following list of statements', or it might simply be made up of a list of positive and negative statements which respondents are asked to tick.

Ethical issues in research design

The British Sociological Association (BSA) suggests a number of ethical guidelines that should be adopted when doing sociological research:

- The well-being, rights and interests of the respondent must be protected.
- Informed consent should be sought.
- The research must be done on the basis of free participation and withdrawal.
- Confidentiality, privacy and anonymity should be guaranteed.
- Researchers need to consider the effects of the research on the respondents.
- Pseudonyms should be used.
- People who are ill, very young, very elderly or frail should be treated with special consideration.

The BSA is particularly concerned about the use of ethnographic methods such as covert observation because such methods involve a degree of deception: the researcher hides his or her true identity and consequently people are misled. The BSA is not keen on this method and recommends that if it is used, the subjects of the

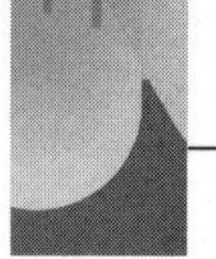

research should be informed about the research when it has been concluded and their consent should be sought at that stage.

Other ethical considerations

- Research can be ethically compromising because it may involve receiving information about criminal activities.
- Sometimes the research focus of the sociological study has the potential to cause anxiety, upset and grief and needs to be sensitively handled.
- Some sociologists believe that taking ethical risks is worthwhile because it may be the only valid way of gaining access to the data needed.

Key concepts

operationalisation; hypothesis; ethics; social class; ethnicity

Methodological techniques: primary methods

Primary methods of research generate new data or knowledge, while secondary methods use evidence that has already been gathered by another researcher or organisation. Some studies use a combination of both types of data-gathering.

Surveys

The social or sample survey is the most popular research method. It normally involves the random selection of a representative large-scale sample. This sample may be sent standardised questionnaires through the post and/or asked to take part in structured interviews in order to obtain quantitative (or sometimes qualitative) data. Surveys generally document opinions or attitudes, but some aim to identify correlations and make causal links. The survey has a number of strengths:

(1) If sampling is carried out without bias, i.e. randomly, and questionnaires are objectively designed, the social survey is the sociological equivalent of the laboratory method because all variables are controlled.

(2) It is a highly reliable method because it is easily repeated and verified.

(3) It is seen to be objective because the sample population is randomly rather than deliberately selected.

(4) It generates lots of quantifiable data, i.e. statistics, in a relatively short period of time and relatively cheaply compared with other methods.

Longitudinal surveys

This type of survey is sometimes called a 'panel study' or a 'cohort study' and goes on for a number of years.

- The key advantage of this approach is that it can reflect social change within the sample. The researcher will return to the group at set intervals, and life patterns can be analysed.
- A longitudinal survey provides an in-depth and therefore qualitative picture of a group or social trends.
- Regular contact over years can create trust and rapport between a group and the researchers and produce more valid data than those generated by one-off questionnaires or interviews.

Survey questionnaires

A questionnaire is a set of questions on paper (though internet or e-mail versions are increasingly common), which respondents are asked to complete. Data are gathered by means of fixed questions or items such as lists of statements with which people are asked to agree or disagree. Questionnaires are normally standardised, i.e. everyone who fills in the questionnaire is exposed to the same questions or statements. They may be composed of:

- closed questions — responses are listed and fixed for the respondent to tick
- open questions — the response is not restricted to pre-set categories; the respondent can respond freely
- ranking questions — respondents are asked to rank items in order of importance
- attitudinal questions — respondents scale their responses, e.g. 'strongly agree', 'disagree' etc.
- multiple choice questions — respondents are asked to tick statements that reflect their experience

Designing a questionnaire

Researchers try to avoid certain types of question in order not to undermine the validity of their data:

- ambiguous questions — each question must be open to one interpretation alone and must have the same meaning for all people taking part
- loaded questions — emotional or sensitive questions may provoke negative and invalid responses
- leading questions — the respondent must not be directed to give a particular response by the wording of the question
- presuming questions — it should not be assumed that the respondent thinks or does something
- double questions — two separate questions require separate answers and should not be combined
- technical questions — technical jargon may not be understood
- vague questions — terms like 'generally', 'sometimes', 'seldom' mean different things to different people

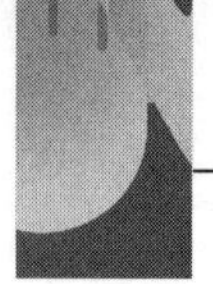

Key concepts

social survey; variables; standardisation; objectivity; quantifiability; longitudinal; panel study; cohort study; open and closed questions; response rate; leading and loaded questions

Strengths of survey questionnaires

- Surveys allow large amounts of data to be collected at a relatively low cost.
- Questionnaires can be distributed over a large geographical area and, if the sampling method adopted is efficient, they can be highly representative of the population, therefore giving a national or community picture.
- Some sociologists regard large surveys as offering high levels of reliability because they are scientific in nature and expose respondents to the same standardised stimulus.
- The anonymity of respondents can be ensured, thus improving the response rate, especially if the study involves a sensitive topic.
- Once the questionnaire has been distributed, the sociologist cannot influence the respondent.
- If the items are pre-coded, the results are quite easy to analyse and tabulate and therefore have comparative value.

Weaknesses of survey questionnaires

- Many questionnaire surveys, especially the postal variety, suffer from very low response rates because there is no motivation for respondents to send them back.
- Sociologists often criticise this method because it does not allow the respondent to explain his or her experiences, motives, etc. to the researcher in any significant detail.
- Respondents might misunderstand items, no matter how carefully they have been designed, and this may lower the validity of the survey.
- With postal questionnaires, it is difficult to verify the identity of the person completing the form.
- The sample in a longitudinal survey may move away, die or refuse to take part the longer the study goes on. For example, many of the original sample involved in the television survey *Seven Up!* have now dropped out.

Studies that have used the survey method include *Poverty in the UK* (1979) by Peter Townsend, which did a great deal to convince people that poverty had not been abolished in the affluent 1960s as many believed. *A Nation of Home Owners* (1990) by Peter Saunders examined the growth of owner–occupancy in the UK and the implications for society, and *Social Class in Modern Britain* (1988) by Gordon Marshall et al. took a random sample of 1,315 adults in the UK and asked questions about social class, attitudes and behaviour.

Interviews

Interviews are clearly related to questionnaires, but are different in key respects. The relationship between researcher and respondent in interviews is face-to-face.

- **Structured or formal interviews** use an interview schedule on which fixed, pre-coded items are written. The items are standardised for all respondents and allow no freedom for the researcher to elaborate or make changes. The researcher records the answers given by the respondent. This could be done manually, or it could involve the use of a tape recorder (though some respondents are uncomfortable about their responses being recorded). If the latter approach is taken, it is necessary to transcribe the responses onto a recording sheet later.
- **Unstructured or informal interviews** involve the interviewer using a series of headings which mark out the main areas to explore in the interview. These will usually be worded as informal, open-ended questions. In addition to these questions researchers will use 'prompts' which aim to move the discussion into interesting areas arising from comments made by the respondent. The interviewee can respond freely and in depth; the sociologist's own priorities or interpretations should not be imposed on the interview. Trust and rapport can be developed because the respondent can see that his or her input is valued and this may generate more qualitative and valid information. Unstructured interviews also allow the researcher to probe for deeper meanings. In many ways this style of interviewing is like a guided conversation, in which the respondent can shape (to some degree) the direction the interview takes.
- **Semi-structured interviews** tend to be made up of a combination of closed questions, usually gaining factual information about the respondent, and open questions, usually aimed at eliciting attitudinal information.

The strengths of interviews

- Interviews ensure a good response rate, provided rapport and trust is established.
- Personal and sensitive areas of experience can be researched, and detailed information can be gathered in semi-structured and unstructured interviews.
- Deviant groups, which are not open to study by other methods, may respond positively to unstructured interviews because they have a chance to present their own viewpoint.
- High levels of validity are obtained from unstructured interview data because sociologists are gathering first-hand accounts and interpretations.
- The researcher can elaborate on areas for discussion in semi-structured and unstructured interviews if the respondent seeks clarification.

The weaknesses of interviews

- Interviews can be time-consuming, especially if semi-structured or unstructured.
- Interviewing can be expensive because interviewers need to be recruited, trained and paid.
- Research using interviews generally involves small samples (because of the expense and the time-consuming nature of this method), so generalisations to wider populations may not be possible because of the unrepresentative nature of interview samples.
- Inaccurate and incomplete recording of respondent comments can mean unreliable research and invalid findings.

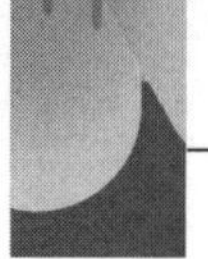

Focus-group interviews

Focus-group interviews have recently become popular with sociologists. These are a type of group interview made up of between four and ten people led by a 'facilitator' or leader who guides the topic being discussed with questions worked out beforehand. Focus-group members are encouraged to respond to each other rather than to the facilitator, thus allowing people to explore their attitudes and experiences in their own words. Such groups also include an 'observer' who notes the organisation of the room and the dynamics of the interaction.

The strengths of focus group interviews

- If facilitators are skilled at group management, trust and rapport should be achieved in a comfortable environment which produces valid data.
- Focus groups not only measure the extent of an opinion, but can also investigate the reasons why it was formed.
- Focus groups result in qualitative data expressed in the words of the participants.

The weaknesses of focus-group interviews

- Focus groups are not generally representative of particular social groups.
- Focus groups may not be representative of the general population because strong personalities may dominate and silence dissent.

Interview bias or effect

All types of interview suffer from bias or effect, which can affect the validity of data. This may take several forms:

(1) A power imbalance is automatically built into a social situation where one person interviews another, which may undermine the validity of research findings. For example, some people may find interviews threatening because they are not sure about the motives of the interviewer. Others may associate interviewers with officialdom, authority and possible punishment and consequently might not cooperate fully and withhold information.

(2) The interviewer's social identity and status may affect the interview process. Ethnicity, age, sex and even social class (demonstrated by accent or dress) may play a part in how well the interview goes. For example, teenagers may interpret adult interviewers asking about aspects of illegal delinquent behaviour as threatening and consequently fail to cooperate fully.

(3) Even those who do not feel threatened by the research will search for clues from the interviewer and the questions about how they ought to be behaving. These 'demand characteristics' may mean that respondents adjust their behaviour in order to influence the way in which the interviewer sees them.

(4) The 'social desirability' effect is one effect of demand characteristics. It involves the over-reporting of 'desirable' things such as giving to charity and the under-reporting of 'undesirable' things such as racist behaviour.

(5) Another problem with interviews arises from human nature. Many people engage in yea-saying — tending to agree rather than disagree, to be satisfied rather than dissatisfied etc.

(6) When interviews are carried out the researcher needs to pay careful attention and be sensitive to non-verbal communication cues such as body language which reveal the reaction of the respondent to the issues being discussed. The body language of the interviewer may also reveal a particular viewpoint on an issue and affect the validity of the interviewee's response. Researchers should attempt to strike a neutral position on the topics being discussed.

(7) The location of the interview needs to be one in which all respondents feel comfortable and should not be too formal.

Key concepts

structured interviews; unstructured interviews; interviewer bias or effect; validity; focus groups; subjectivity; bias; social identity; social desirability effect; yea-saying; demand characteristics

Studies that have used interviews include *Homeworking Women* (Phizacklea and Wolkowicz 1995) which examined aspects of daily home-based work for women from various ethnicities in different types of job. The *Living with Heroin* study (Parker et al. 1988) used interviews to find out why young people in the Wirrall used heroin.

Pilot studies

Most of the problems with questionnaires and interviews can be minimised by carrying out a pilot study. This small-scale prototype of the main study can act as a 'dress rehearsal' and provide guidance on the following areas:

- whether the sampling frame is suitable
- the potential non-response from the target audience
- the clarity of the questionnaire or interview schedule
- whether the questions should be open or closed, e.g. in order to collect all possible answers for a closed question in the main survey, the researcher could have open questions in the pilot
- the effectiveness of the interviewers

Observation methods

Direct observation

With this method the researcher 'stands outside' the group or social situation being studied and works 'at a distance'. The aim is to get inside the heads of those being studied and to see the world through their eyes. This is *verstehen*, whereby the researcher intends to empathise with those being studied, to understand their motives, their attitudes and the social interpretations they attach to everyday life. For example, a sociologist might be interested in how people behave in everyday contexts such as bus queues.

Some observers use an observation schedule or tally-chart which is a list of categories of behaviour the sociologist expects to see in support of the hypothesis. Sometimes observers use observation grids or sociograms to map out interactions or patterns of friendship between people. These categories and grids operationalise the hypothesis.

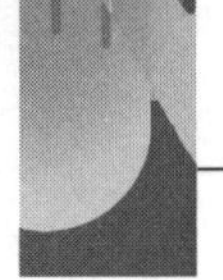

- Observation allows the researcher some access to the world of the group being studied and is therefore what sociologists call an ethnographic approach.
- Most sociologists who have used this method usually carry out a pilot observation to identify the 'fields' or categories of observation, i.e. what specific aspects of the situation are most worthy of study.
- The pilot observation will help determine how much factual detail to record about members of the group being observed (e.g. age, sex) and what names or numbers to give to them so that their behaviour can be recorded effectively.
- Once the research has been carried out, the sociologist's urgent task is to analyse the recorded details whilst images and memories are still fresh in the mind.

The strengths of observation

- This method is regarded as producing valid data because the researcher is detached from 'the action' and is therefore unlikely to affect and distort the group's behaviour.
- Observation operates in the natural environment of those being studied. In this sense, it is less artificial than questionnaires or interviews.
- People may not be aware that they are behaving in certain ways. Questionnaires and interviews can only uncover conscious behaviour, while observation may reveal people acting in ways that they would deny if asked directly.
- The researcher is unlikely to lose objectivity because of the detached nature of this method.

The weaknesses of observation

- Observation is time-consuming — research of this nature often takes months, even years.
- The selectivity of the researcher can present problems. A vast amount of behaviour is observed and the sociologist has to make decisions about which behaviour does or does not support the research hypothesis, opening the way for accusations of bias.
- However well access to the group has been managed, the presence of a researcher may disrupt the natural behaviour of the group and create artificial reactions. This is known as the Hawthorne effect after a famous observation conducted in the 1930s at the Hawthorne plant of the General Electric Company in which it was realised that workers were working harder because they were being observed.
- Some aspects of group behaviour may be difficult to interpret or understand, especially if the sociologist is not involved in the group.
- The sociologist's interpretation of the data may be compromised by the fact that he or she likes the group and therefore is unable to judge their actions objectively.

Key concepts

ethnography; participant observation; covert observation; pilot observation; demand characteristics; sociogram; *verstehen*

Participant observation

Participant observation is where the sociologist actually joins the social group being studied. Many sociologists claim that this method has a high level of validity because the sociologist experiences first hand the worldview of those he or she is studying.

Participant observation is usually the only way of obtaining detailed information about groups that traditionally 'shut out' or exclude social researchers, e.g. deviant groups whose members follow a lifestyle and subscribe to a value-system that is very different from and possibly opposed to mainstream values.

There are two broad types of participant observation:

(1) Overt participant observation is when the sociologist spends extended periods of time living with a group but has made it clear to its members that she or he is not a 'standard' group-member, and does not want to adopt the style of the group or its values, but is simply a person doing some research. This type of participant observation permits questions to be asked about the way the group does things whenever new situations arise. The researcher has 'owned up' to the fact that she or he is an outsider, so questions are not out of place. Equally, the researcher is at liberty to record openly things she or he considers of sociological significance, and the group members will not see this as odd. This type of participant observation has one major drawback: the presence of a researcher within the group may distort or inhibit the group's behaviour.

(2) Covert participant observation involves living with a group, but this time the sociologist 'goes undercover' and hides the fact that she or he is doing research. This has the advantage of allowing the sociologist to study the group when its members are behaving naturally and therefore increases the validity of data collected. However, the researcher has a great deal of learning to do in order to fit into the group. The body language, style of dress, slang or language, customs and rituals of the group will have to be learned. Many sociologists gain access to groups through an intermediary — somebody who can vouch for them. Once access has been gained the researcher faces the challenge of recording events effectively without raising suspicions.

Strengths of participant observation

- Participant observation allows access to 'exclusive' data and natural behaviour in contrast with other methods which produce more artificial behaviour.
- Participant observation data, especially when gathered by covert observation, result in high levels of validity because people are behaving naturally.
- Participant observation often gives rise to new ideas for study as a direct result of researchers being involved with groups.
- Because the research is ongoing, it gives a picture of the group as dynamic (changing) rather than static, which adds a special quality and validity to the information gathered.

Weaknesses of participant observation

- Participant observation can be extremely time-consuming and expensive — some studies have lasted for 5 years.

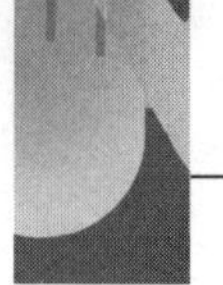

- There can be ethical problems because there is a risk of the researcher being drawn into illegal behaviour when studying criminal groups — the question arises whether the researcher should 'break cover' and refuse to participate or stay covert and hope the behaviour does not get too deviant.
- Researchers conducting observations can be exposed to danger.
- Another ethical problem is that 'informed consent' is not obtained from those being observed, and many argue that this makes the sociologist guilty of deceiving respondents and betraying their trust.
- If people know they are being watched this may produce artificial behaviour.
- There is also the danger that researchers can become too involved in the life of the group. Some sociologists have been known to 'go native' and lose their sense of objectivity, therefore potentially lowering the validity of any data gathered.
- Some sociologists argue that the reliability of observation is low because it is not based on a standardised scientific approach. Rather it is dependent upon the strength of the unique personal relationships that the researcher establishes with those being observed, which cannot be replicated by other sociologists.
- Participant observation studies tend to focus on small, exotic or deviant groups which may not be representative of society, so generalisability may be low (although observation studies are often presented as case studies which do not aim to generalise).
- Final conclusions are always based on the subjective and selective interpretations of a single researcher who chooses what to include in the published findings.

Key concepts

ethnography; participant observation; covert observation; sociogram; reflexivity; objectivity; Hawthorne effect; going native

Methodological techniques: secondary data

Sociologists also use secondary data, i.e. information gathered by other sociologists or organisations. This pre-existing data can take a number of forms.

Official statistics

These are figures collected by government or state agencies. They are an example of quantitative data and are gathered through surveys by both national and local government agencies. They offer the sociologist a rich data bank to tap into and cover a range of aspects of the way we live as a society.

Generally speaking, official statistics are divided into two categories: registration data and survey data.

Registration data

This involves the recording (as a continuous process) of sociologically important events such as births, deaths, marriages and divorces. The UK has a highly developed system of registering, documenting and quantifying key social events. For example, the Department for Education and Skills (DfES) records truancy rates in schools in England and Wales.

Survey data

This type of official statistic is gathered by social surveys which happen at particular times. These are often huge surveys of representative samples.

- The best example is the decennial census. Every 10 years millions of questionnaires are filled in and valuable data gathered about life in Britain. The last census was in 2001 and it cost £254 million.
- On a more frequent basis, the *General Household Survey* and the *New Earnings Survey* provide annual information. Much of the data gathered by such surveys can be found in *Social Trends*. The *British Crime Survey* gathers information about how much crime has been reported by victims and is often used to cross-check the accuracy of the official criminal statistics, which are made up of crimes reported to the police, crimes detected and convictions in the courts.

Strengths of official statistics

- Official statistics are extremely easy and cheap to access.
- Official statistics are up to date.
- They are often gathered by surveys which involve huge, carefully constructed representative samples and therefore can be generalised for similar populations.
- Positivists see official statistics as 'hard' reliable facts because they have been collected in a standardised, systematic and scientific fashion.
- Trends can be identified by comparing official statistics from regularly conducted surveys, e.g. the census.

Weaknesses of official statistics

- Many official statistics do not 'speak for themselves' — they raise serious questions about reliability and validity.
- Official statistics may only give us a partial picture of a sociological problem. For example, the official crime statistics do not include unreported and undetected crimes.
- Official statistics may tell us more about the people involved in their collection than the social trend they claim to describe. For example, crime statistics may tell us more about police and judicial practices than about criminality, while suicide statistics may tell us more about social attitudes towards suicide and the practices of coroners than the motives of suicide victims.
- Statistics are one-dimensional in their validity, i.e. they tell us very little about the human stories or interpretations that underpin them.
- Official statistics are open to political abuse — they can be manipulated or 'massaged' by governments for political advantage. For example, the validity of unemployment and NHS waiting-list statistics may be undermined by frequent re-definitions by government or selective practices.

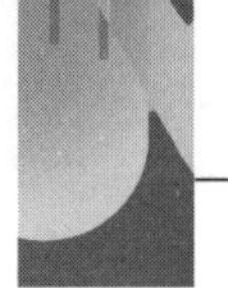

- Official statistics may be based on operational definitions that sociologists would not agree with. For example, the government may use absolute ways of defining poverty based on income levels whereas sociologists may prefer relative approaches to measuring poverty.

Studies that have used this source include *Suicide* (Durkheim 1897), a classic study that used a comparative approach to identify different types of suicide and the variables that predisposed members of social groups to this act. *A Nation of Home Owners* (Saunders 1990) used statistics to examine the growth of owner-occupancy in the UK and the implications for society.

Key concepts

case study; methodological pluralism; official statistics; registration data; survey data; the census

Personal or expressive documents

Sociologists often try to gain access to the personal or expressive documents which record people's social experiences, e.g. letters and personal diaries.

- Such 'life documents' offer the researcher a potentially rich source of qualitative data and an insight into the life history of an individual or group.
- These types of data can reveal the emotions, reflections and motivations of the research subjects, i.e. they are likely to be high in validity.
- Diaries and letters can give significant insight as people go through challenging social experiences such as bereavement.
- They are favoured by the interpretive branch of sociology. Some feminist writers also consider them to be valuable.
- The sociologist should always obtain consent from the person who wrote the letters or diary (unless the person is deceased).

Strengths of personal documents

- Personal documents give rich, detailed and valid insight into challenging social experiences and emotions.
- They often give insight over a long period of time, so social change can be examined.
- They are often the only insight sociologists have into the past.

Weaknesses of personal documents

- The validity of data offered by such sources may be undermined by doubts about the documents' authenticity.
- There is selectivity in what the writer includes in such documents. Writers of diaries or letters are unlikely to include information that may prejudice the reader against them.
- Analysing such documents introduces a further degree of subjectivity. There is always the danger that the sociologist will interpret what a writer is saying in a different way to that which the writer intended.

- Such documents are not produced with sociological research in mind, so they may offer only a partial insight into the lifestyle in question.
- The experiences described are unlikely to be typical or representative because there is a tendency for only certain types of people, e.g. literary, political people in the public eye, to keep letters or write diaries about their experiences.

Studies which have used this approach include *The Polish Peasant in Europe and America* (Thomas and Znaniecki 1919), a classic study of migration to the United States, and *The Company She Keeps* (Hey 1997), a study of girls' friendships through their diaries and notes to each other. Students might also wish to refer to *Documents of Life* (Plummer 1983).

Key concepts

life documents; expressive documents; consent; qualitative; authenticity

Contemporary documents

Media products, such as newspapers, magazines, advertisements, radio, music products, posters, films, novels, internet and computer products, tell us something about the society in which we live. Sociologists often use media extracts or items to reflect society's values and concerns at any point in time. Equally, quality investigative journalism can generate reliable evidence which may complement the research of the sociologist.

Content analysis

This is a type of secondary method as it involves working with secondary data, but can also be seen as a primary method as it generates new knowledge. It involves the analysis of patterns or 'messages' in the mass media and can generate both quantitative and qualitative data. The sociologist can work with any form of media product, e.g. newspapers, television programmes or magazines, and also with other cultural products such as novels. The aim of the research, in general, is to identify how particular social groups or social situations are portrayed in the product. There are a number of key elements to content analysis :

- The quantitative form of this method involves a 'tallying' or counting approach and uses a grid that records the patterns and frequency of certain images. For example, a sociologist studying images of masculinity and femininity in the workplace as depicted in Australian soap operas on television will systematically record frequencies of images, representations, categories etc.
- The qualitative form of this method, known as semiology or textual analysis, involves analysing language, images, narrative etc. for ideological content, i.e. asking whether the product reflects a dominant political or cultural position. Semiologists argue that these ideological messages might be about femininity, national pride or race, but whatever they deal with, they are subconsciously absorbed by society in everyday 'reading' of images and words.

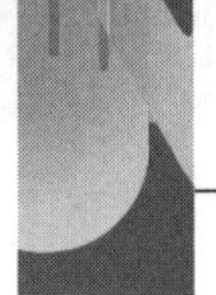

- The sociologist needs to select the sample carefully. The selection of, say, particular magazines or television programmes needs to be justified. For example, a researcher looking at television advertising needs to think very carefully about which channels are to be sampled, at what time of day etc.

Strengths of media content analysis

- Media products are interesting and useful to the sociologist if treated with caution.
- They are cheap and readily available.
- The method of content analysis, whether it is the tallying or semiotic kind, is not very costly.
- If a longitudinal comparative version is used, it allows the sociologist to compare depictions and representations over a period of time.

Weaknesses of media content analysis

- Media products can be unreliable because they may reflect the personal and political prejudices of for example journalists, editors and media owners.
- The content of these products is not constructed or designed with sociological research in mind and may lack sociological precision.
- Content analysis is very time-consuming.
- Semiotics can be highly subjective, largely depending upon the interpretation of the researcher.
- Sociologists who have used this method have been accused of taking an image or set of words out of context and misinterpreting the meaning.
- Using this method often means assuming that these media images etc. have an effect upon their audience. However, there is no proof of this.

Studies which have used this method include *Bad News* (1976) by the Glasgow Media Group, which suggested that industrial disputes and business matters are reported in a biased way, and *Forever Feminine* (Ferguson 1983), which detailed various images of femininity in magazines.

Key concepts

content analysis; semiology; textual analysis; tallying; ideological content

Triangulation

Triangulation can be defined as the use of more than one research method in order to assess the validity of the research and data produced. This usually involves using a method which generates quantitative data alongside a method which generates qualitative data. The advantages of this approach include:

- It can be used to check the accuracy of the data gathered by each method. For example, questionnaires or structured interviews can be artificial or impersonal and tend not to produce wholly honest or open answers. The use of a qualitative device alongside these, e.g. unstructured interviews with a sub-sample, serves to cross-check the validity of people's responses.
- Qualitative research can produce hypotheses which can be checked and researched using quantitative methods.

- The two approaches can give a more complete picture of the group being studied, i.e. they can be studied from a number of different angles.
- Qualitative research can focus on the 'why' and 'how' of the trends uncovered by statistics. For example, research on divorce can uncover both statistical trends and people's actual feelings about the experience of divorce.

Eileen Barker's *The Making of a Moonie* (1984) (a study of a religious sect) is a good example of triangulation in practice.

Methodological pluralism

Methodological pluralism refers to the employment of more than one research method, normally in a two-stage study in which both methods are given equal status. The emphasis is on building up a fuller and more comprehensive picture of social life by generating different types of data which shed light on different parts of the research problem. This differs from the classic form of triangulation which aims primarily to use one method in order to cross-check data from another.

Janet Finch and Jennifer Mason's *Negotiating Family Responsibilities* (1993) (which examined how family members supported each other) is a good example of methodological pluralism in practice.

Strengths of multiple methods

- Triangulation and methodological pluralism are useful because the advantages of one method may help compensate for the limitations of another.
- There are few areas of social life where one research method alone is sufficient to gain a meaningful insight into people's lives.

Weaknesses of multiple methods

- These approaches are expensive.
- They produce vast amounts of data which can be difficult to analyse.
- The nature of the topic to be investigated dictates which method(s) are employed and rules out others.

Case studies

When a sociologist uses the case study approach it is usually in order to study in depth a particular organisation, a group, or an individual.

With an organisational case study, the sociologist might study an organisation with the aim of getting inside the 'life' of the institution using methodological pluralism. For example, for a case study of a factory, the sociologist might interview the shop-floor workers to find out about their levels of loyalty to the company, and use participant observation to record incidents of conflict between workers and management, as well as issuing a questionnaire to a sample of employees at all levels in order to establish levels of job satisfaction. Once all of these data were analysed and interpreted, the sociologist would have a comprehensive insight into the social life of the organisation.

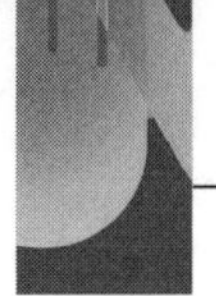

The other type of case study involves in-depth analysis of the experiences and views of a small sample of individuals with similar experiences, e.g. people who had all been victims of violent crime in order to find out how respondents had altered their lifestyles as a result of their experiences. Semi-structured interviews could be used. The case-study approach usually necessitates repeated interviews, over a period of time, which gives more depth and also the possibility of recording changes over time. The sociologist might try to gain access to personal documents, e.g. letters and diaries, that might give insight into the life experiences of the respondents, or might ask people to keep diaries recording their fears about crime.

Strengths of case studies

- Case studies often result in a high degree of insight into people's experiences and emotions.
- They are relatively cheap to carry out.
- The case study stresses the viewpoints and interpretations of those being studied and therefore scores highly in terms of validity.

Weaknesses of case studies

- The organisation or group being studied may not be representative of society as a whole, so generalisation may not be possible (although sociologists conducting case studies often argue that their aims are quite different from those involved in a social survey).
- The reliability of data is sometimes questionable, especially when respondents are asked to remember past events.

Key concepts

case-study; cross-checking; methodological pluralism; triangulation

Questions & Answers

This section of the guide provides you with three examination papers (made up of two compulsory questions plus four optional questions) on the topic of Exploring Social Inequality and Difference in the style of the OCR examination. These are followed by examples of grade-A responses to most of the questions in the first two papers. Some of these grade-A responses are accompanied by grade-C responses — you should compare the differences between these in order to work out how to improve the quality of your own responses.

It is important to note that these are not 'model' answers. They are not the only possible answers to these questions, nor are they necessarily the best. They represent one particular successful style; one that answers the question and demonstrates the appropriate skills, especially using suitable concepts and studies, displaying a critical and evaluative awareness towards the material used, and presenting a logically structured argument.

Do not make the mistake of learning the grade-A responses parrot-fashion. Remember that you have to be flexible and you have to be able to respond to the specific demands of a question. It would be quite possible, particularly in the answers to Option 1 and 2 (a) and (b), to take a different approach and still gain very high marks.

A third paper is provided which is accompanied by a plan of action. You should use this to write your own response. It is recommended that you spend some time revising the topic before tackling this question. You should answer the question under timed conditions with no notes.

Examiner's comments

The candidate answers are accompanied by examiner's comments. These are preceded by the icon *e* and indicate where credit is due. For the grade-A answers, the examiner shows you what it is that enables the candidate to score so highly. Particular attention is given to the candidate's use of the examinable skills: knowledge and understanding; interpretation and analysis; and evaluation. For the grade-C answers, the examiner points out areas for improvement, specific problems and common errors. You are also invited to rewrite the answer in order to gain higher marks, and some pointers are given to show you how you might do this.

Cultural capital and social exclusion

Read Item A and answer questions 1 and 2, and then answer either Option 1, 3(a) and 3(b) OR Option 2, 4(a) and 4(b).

Item A

It is argued by Bourdieu that the middle classes have access to cultural capital and this gives them advantages in a middle-class dominated education system. In contrast, working-class culture lacks cultural capital and this places them at a disadvantage in the education system. Bourdieu argues that this lack of cultural capital is the main cause of class inequality in capitalist societies. Savage et al. note that Bourdieu's claims have never been explicitly tested in the UK using both quantitative and qualitative research. Savage et al. therefore designed a piece of research which had two main aims:

- To find out what the nature of cultural capital is in the UK.
- To investigate how important cultural capital is compared with economic and social capital.

The research set out to measure cultural capital by examining how different social classes operate in 'cultural fields', i.e. in terms of their tastes in and attitudes towards music, reading, film, TV, sports, art, leisure, eating out.

The researchers established 25 focus groups, carried out 60 in-depth interviews and conducted a national survey of 1,564 respondents. In order to obtain a sample that was representative of multicultural Britain the survey sample was boosted by an additional 200 people from ethnic minority backgrounds.

Cultural capital was operationalised in a number of ways. Questions focused on eight cultural subfields which aimed to tap into people's tastes, knowledge of and participation in:

- TV — stations watched, programmes (dis)liked, frequency of viewing
- film — genres and directors (dis)liked, frequency of cinema attendance
- music — genres and artists (dis)liked, attendance at musical events
- reading — genres and writers (dis)liked, books read
- visual arts — genres and artists (dis)liked, works possessed
- eating out — kind of venues (dis)liked
- embodiment — sport, body modification, clothes, household style

In addition, questions were asked about economic and social 'capital'; how the domestic division of labour in their households was organised; parents' cultural interests and background and the respondents' social, cultural and political attitudes.

paper

The research found that class divisions are still profound with regard to consumption, lifestyle and therefore, cultural capital. The evidence suggests that Britain has three fairly strongly culturally bounded classes — the service, intermediate and working class. However, the research also discovered that age (and to a lesser extent, gender and ethnicity) prove to be of fundamental importance in shaping cultural practices.

Adapted from Savage, M., Warde, A. and Devine, F. (2005) 'Capitals, assets, and resources: some critical issues', *The British Journal of Sociology* 56 (1): pp. 31–47.

Compulsory questions

1 Using the item and your own knowledge outline and explain how social surveys are used in sociological research. (15 marks)

2 Outline and assess the claim made by some sociologists that unstructured interviews produce more valid data than structured interviews with regard to investigating cultural capital. (25 marks)

Then answer either:

Option 1

3 (a) Outline the evidence that challenges the view that 'we are all middle class now'. (20 marks)

(b) Assess sociological explanations of the view that the changing nature of employment is having significant effects on class boundaries. (40 marks)

OR

Option 2

4 (a) Outline the evidence that social class inequalities exist in the contemporary UK. (20 marks)

(b) Assess Marxist theories of stratification. (40 marks)

Answer to compulsory question 1: grade-C candidate

Using the item and your own knowledge outline and explain how social surveys are used in sociological research.

The social survey is the most common way that sociologists gather data. It normally involves collecting lots of statistical data from a large number of people in a relatively short space of time. This data is collected using questionnaires although structured interviews are also sometimes used. Sometimes these questionnaires are handed out by hand or they may be sent through the post or even posted on the internet. The whole point of surveys is to collect statistics which can then be compared against a hypothesis to work out whether something is true or not.

e **A reasonably successful opening paragraph which clearly identifies the constituent parts of the survey method although the final sentence needs to be more precise, e.g. an example could have been used to illustrate this point.**

Surveys usually involve the collection of samples — these are groups of people who have agreed to take part in the survey. Surveys are liked by positivist sociologists who think that this method is very reliable because it is repeatable. The same survey can be done in different parts of the country and it produces national statistics telling the sociologist how people living in different areas behave.

e **The candidate makes a satisfactory point about positivism but the explanation about why surveys are reliable is lacking in detail. It needs to go beyond the notion of 'repeatability'. The point about surveys and different parts of the country is over-simplistic.**

Surveys usually use questionnaires made up of two types of questions. Some use closed questions in which people are asked to tick boxes which list 4–5 possible responses. Some use open questions which mean that people are not restricted by boxes. Some surveys use a combination of both closed and open questions. It is really important that questions are designed in a way that reduces bias. For example, some questions are so poorly designed that they are loaded. This means that they will upset people and therefore they may not want to answer. Leading questions make people give the answers that the researcher wants to hear.

e **Most of the information in this paragraph is relevant but it tends to be simplistic in terms of both explanation and illustration. Some explanation is not accurate enough, e.g. the definition of loaded questions needs to be more precise and illustration is required for the concept of leading questions.**

Surveys allow large amounts of data to be collected at a relatively low cost. In Savage's study they were able to send out over 1,000 questionnaires over the whole of the UK. This should make the method very representative especially as they also included ethnic minority people. They filled in the same questionnaire as the white people and therefore this makes the survey reliable.

e **The candidate makes a reasonable comment about the cost of surveys. We also see the first reference to the study mentioned in the source material although what the candidate says about the study needs greater accuracy and detail, e.g. the cultural capital survey questioned 1,764 people rather than 'over 1,000'. The link to reliability is also very weak.**

They probably increased the validity of the answers they received by telling everybody who took part that they could remain anonymous because cultural capital is a very sensitive topic that people prefer not to talk about. There is also the danger with questionnaires that they suffer from very poor response rates. People might also not understand the questions which will affect the reliability of the results. They might also get their children to fill in the questionnaire because they have not got the time.

e This is a poor paragraph full of gross over-simplifications. It is not clear why cultural capital might be regarded as a 'sensitive' topic or why questionnaires suffer from very poor response rates. The candidate also confuses reliability with validity. The point of the last sentence is not made clear at all.

A very important part of surveys is sampling and operationalisation. Sampling can either be random or non-random although random is more likely for questionnaires involving large numbers of people. Random sampling involves choosing people to take part in the survey by getting a computer to randomly choose the names of people. There are different types, e.g. stratified sampling involves breaking the research population down into groups such as age groups, social classes, ethnic groups, and there are signs that the research on cultural capital did this because they used a booster sample of 200 ethnic minorities.

e The points made about sampling are satisfactory rather than insightful. The reference to stratified sampling is accurate and the candidate does attempt to link it to the research in the source material.

Operationalisation is when the researcher takes their hypothesis — the thing they are attempting to test to see if it is true or wrong — and turns it into a series of questions. The statistics that result from these questions can be turned into tables and graphs, and compared with the hypothesis to see whether it supports what the researcher believes or whether it contradicts it. It is therefore very important that the data is reliably collected and that everybody understands the questions in the same way otherwise the data will not be true or valid.

e The definition of operationalisation and the points that follow about statistics, tables, graphs etc. are satisfactory. The paragraph finishes with the intelligent and accurate observation that collection of data must be reliable and that questions need to be interpreted in the same way by all respondents if data are to be valid.

Overall this candidate makes some satisfactory observations about surveys. There is reasonably good knowledge and understanding. However, lack of illustrative detail lets the candidate down as does the failure to get to grips in any real detail with the survey focused upon by the source material. This candidate therefore would probably score 5/10 for knowledge and understanding, i.e. there is a reasonably good understanding of the purpose of social surveys and what is referred to is appropriate.

However, the candidate makes only one reference to the source material. Moreover, there is no reference to theory which is a necessity at A2. The candidate would probably score 3/5 for interpretation and analysis, i.e. there is a good ability to interpret sociological knowledge but illustrative exemplars would be required to score higher. This candidate therefore would gain 8 marks out of a possible 15.

Answer to compulsory question 1: grade-A candidate

Using the item and your own knowledge outline and explain how social surveys are used in sociological research.

The social survey is the most commonly used sociological research method. It usually involves randomly selecting a sample of people or respondents from the research population the sociologist is interested in studying. The idea is that the sample mirrors the research population in terms of their social characteristics. The sample will have a questionnaire distributed to it by hand, or by post or even via e-mail or a posting on a website. Sometimes the questionnaire is administered by the researchers themselves in the form of a structured interview.

e A focused and detailed beginning which clearly identifies what constitutes a social survey and how it operates with regard to sampling.

Positivists argue that social surveys are very scientific — they are thought to be a highly reliable method because they are easily repeated and their results verified by other sociologists. They also appeal to positivist sociologists because they produce a lot of quantifiable data, i.e. statistics, which can be compared in order to establish correlations, and even cause and effect relationships, which can be used to support or contradict hypotheses.

e A reasonably good reference to positivism which accurately identifies three principles of this scientific approach to research, i.e. reliability, quantifiability and correlation/cause and effect.

The research in the source above was focused on the concept of cultural capital. The survey designed around this concept was generally descriptive in that it aimed to find out what form cultural capital took in the UK and how it operated alongside both economic and social capital. It was decided to operationalise cultural capital by looking at how different social classes experienced what the researchers called 'cultural fields', i.e. their tastes and attitudes towards music, reading, television, sports, art, leisure, eating out etc. Questions were therefore designed in order to quantify these cultural fields, exploring how often people watched television, went to the cinema, read books and attended musical events or art galleries. Questions focused on people's taste in terms of the television channels and programmes they watched, what their favourite genres and styles of film, music, books and art were and where they liked to go in terms of art galleries, museums, restaurants.

Questions also focused on how the respondents saw sport and whether they saw image as important in terms of their bodies, their clothing and their homes. Finally, economic and social capital were also operationalised by asking questions about how they organised housework and childcare, their parents' social background and cultural tastes, and their social, cultural and political attitudes.

In these two paragraphs, the candidate follows the instructions in the question and uses the source material intelligently and in a detailed fashion. The concept of 'operationalisation' is very impressively discussed with regard to cultural capital. This candidate displays genuine understanding of the concept of cultural capital and the research process.

This research aimed to focus on the differences in behaviour and attitudes between social classes. It is important that sociologists clearly state how this concept is being operationalised. This survey used the NS–SEC, which classifies jobs into eight occupational groupings, which are further reduced into these three broad classes that differ in terms of employment relations and employment or market conditions.

e The candidate successfully identifies how the study in the source operationalises the concept of social class. It might have benefited from further discussion but the candidate has only got about 20 minutes to write about 600 words.

Surveys are seen as advantageous because they allow large amounts of data to be collected at a relatively low cost. The research in the source, for example, conducted a nationwide survey involving 1,764 respondents including a booster sample of 200 people from ethnic minority backgrounds in order that their sample reflected society in general. In addition, the researchers supplemented the quantitative data collected by their surveys by forming 25 focus groups and carrying out 60 in-depth interviews in order to collect qualitative data in terms of attitudes and opinions.

e A clear description of the research in the source material in terms of the sample used and the two types of data generated.

Sociologists often criticise the questionnaire method because it often does not allow the respondent to explain his or her experiences, motives etc. to the researcher in any significant detail. However, the study in the source does supplement the questionnaire with the more qualitative focus group approach.

e An important criticism is supplemented by an understanding of how the use of focus groups might have compensated for the shortcomings of the questionnaire.

Savage's research uses a form of methodological pluralism, i.e. the survey questionnaire probably focused on collecting quantitative data whilst the focus groups concentrated on acquiring qualitative data which probably explained the actions and tastes described by the survey data. The net result of these methods was that Savage confirmed that the service and intermediate classes, i.e. the middle classes, had cultural tastes and lifestyles that significantly differed from the working class. Furthermore, the cultural tastes etc. of the middle classes may give them significant advantages in terms of cultural capital.

e An excellent understanding is demonstrated in this paragraph that Savage's research constitutes a methodological pluralist approach. There is also a reference to the findings of the research.

Overall, this candidate demonstrates an excellent and perceptive knowledge and understanding of the social survey method especially in terms of how it was used practically in the source material research. There was a clear link to theory although perhaps an interpretivist critique could have been woven into the final sections. However, this is a minor criticism of an examination response which focused in an intelligent way on very appropriate knowledge. There was a depth of sociological understanding demonstrated by the use of source material to illustrate aspects of the survey method. There was also an attempt to capture all elements of the sociological approach to research — the theoretical and practical aspects all illustrated the ability of this candidate to think holistically about the research process. The candidate therefore would score 10/10 for knowledge and understanding. 5/5 would be rewarded for interpretation and analysis because this candidate applied theories and concepts convincingly throughout the response, which was always focused on answering the question. Overall the candidate would score the full 15 marks.

Answer to compulsory question 2: grade-C candidate

Outline and assess the claim made by some sociologists that unstructured interviews produce more valid data than structured interviews with regard to investigating cultural capital.

Structured interviews involve the interviewer using an interview schedule which is a list of fixed questions which the interviewer uses to ask everybody they speak to the same questions. Usually the interviewer is not allowed to change the questions. The researcher records the answers given by the respondent.

e A reasonably good introduction to structured interviews which is generally correct.

Unstructured interviews, on the other hand, are much freer. The interviewer does not have a fixed set of questions that they must ask. The questions will be made up on the hoof in order to explore what the researcher is interested in and they will often depend on the previous answer that the person being interviewed has given. These types of interview are therefore more flexible than structured interviews because they allow the person being interviewed to feel that what they are saying is important. This builds up trust and consequently the interviewee may tell the interviewer things that he wouldn't tell anybody. The interviewer is also free to follow the interviewee who might say stuff that the interviewer hadn't thought of.

e This is a good beginning to the response in that the candidate has rightly decided to start by comparing and contrasting the two types of interview. This paragraph suggests a very good understanding of unstructured interviews despite the simplicity of the language used.

If we compare structured interviews with unstructured interviews, we can see that structured interviews have high levels of reliability because everybody who takes part in the research is asked exactly the same questions by a group of interviewers. Unstructured interviews are not very reliable because they depend on the relationship that the interviewer has established. One interviewer might get loads of information but another may be disliked by the interviewee and get very little.

Good points are raised about the concept of reliability, which demonstrates a good understanding.

However, successful unstructured interviews are usually highly valid because the trust and rapport established with the interviewee means the researcher is getting firsthand accounts of whatever the research is about. These types of interview allow the researcher to probe and prompt for deeper meanings and consequently the data is often from the horse's mouth. Structured interview data is not regarded as valid because the questions are fixed, the interviewer normally cannot ask any extra questions in order to explore what the interviewee meant. Interviewees too might get frustrated if they cannot explain themselves or might feel that the questions are irrelevant to their experience of the world.

A reasonably good account of some of the problems of interviews. It deserves credit for its comparative approach but it has missed the opportunity to illustrate these comparative differences with references to cultural capital as instructed in the question.

Structured interviews are great for producing lots of quantitative data about people's social backgrounds and behaviour but this type of data is not so great for producing in-depth information about people's feelings and motives. Unstructured interviews are great for producing qualitative information.

The candidate rightly highlights the comparative difference of quantitative and qualitative data but the paragraph would have benefited from some illustration.

Both these types of interview are better than questionnaires because direct contact ensures a better response rate than questionnaires, especially those sent through the post. Interviews also allow more personal and sensitive areas of experience to be researched although the unstructured interview probably has more advantages than structured interviews to do this.

This paragraph starts to wander off-track because the question is not asking the candidate to compare interviews with questionnaires. The reference to the unstructured interview having more advantages than the structured interview is meaningless without some type of illustration.

Interviews have several problems. They are more time-consuming and expensive than other methods. They also tend to use smaller samples than questionnaires so it is difficult to generalise from interview data to large research populations. The biggest problem with interviews is interviewer bias or effect. People often find interviews threatening and they might feel nervous and reluctant to open up. They may tell lies because they think that whatever information they give might be used against them especially if the subject matter is a sensitive one or they are being asked about criminal or immoral behaviour.

The candidate has now lost focus. He/she is no longer comparing different types of interviews. This paragraph would have been rewarded more highly if it had overtly focused on the similarities of the two types of interview. There is also still no reference to cultural capital.

The interviewer's status may also affect the interview process. The social class of the interviewer as well as their age, ethnicity, accent and gender may influence the interviewees in a negative way. For example, people who interview teenagers should be pretty young themselves because older interviewers may put them off. Some people will say anything to impress the researcher. Body language and room layouts are also important.

This is a weak finish because the candidate has made no explicit reference to structured or unstructured interviews. For example, the candidate could have discussed how unstructured interviews are more likely to overcome the sorts of problems identified above compared with structured interviews.

Overall this candidate has a reasonably detailed knowledge of interviews but this is undermined by two crucial omissions. First, the candidate fails to construct any theoretical framework for the discussion of the two types of interview. The positivist–interpretivist debate is an important element of debate at A2. Second, the candidate fails to make one reference to cultural capital despite that concept being included in the question. Consequently, for knowledge and understanding, the candidate would score only 3/6 — the material was appropriate but not very well focused. The candidate would score only 2/5 because a crucial part of the question — the reference to cultural capital — was ignored. Finally, the candidate would score 7/15 on evaluation and analysis in that he/she demonstrated a reasonably good ability to put together a comparative analysis. Evaluation would have benefited from a theoretical framework and greater detail. It was often a little vague. This candidate therefore would score 12 marks out of a possible 25, i.e. a grade C, for this response.

Answer to compulsory question 2: grade-A candidate

Outline and assess the claim made by some sociologists that unstructured interviews produce more valid data than structured interviews with regard to investigating cultural capital.

Interpretivists argue that sociological research should focus on the meanings that people use to make sense of the social world. Consequently, interpretivist sociologists are interested in methods that are high in validity such as unstructured interviews because they produce qualitative data which documents how the world looks from the point of view of those being studied.

This candidate rightly begins this response by constructing a theoretical framework in which the value of different types of interview can be assessed. The candidate clearly and rightly links unstructured interviews to the interpretivist position.

Interpretivists emphasise validity. They believe that unique and trusting relationships should be established with those being studied so that a true picture of their

paper

lives can be constructed. Unstructured interviews which sometimes last hours are seen as more likely to produce these relationships than structured interviews.

e Unstructured interviews are convincingly linked to the concept of validity.

Unstructured interviews are essentially discussions between the researcher and the subject group which are managed by the researcher using a series of headings to mark out the main points of the subject group's experience that is going to be explored. The researcher therefore uses informal, open-ended questions which are flexible, i.e. they can be changed or adapted depending on the subject's response. Moreover, the researcher will use 'prompts' which aim to move the discussion into interesting areas arising from comments made by the respondent. For example, the interviewer might start by asking questions relating to the subject's experience of economic capital in terms of their living standards and then as the interview develops begin to explore the more complex concepts of cultural capital, i.e. by asking about attitudes and opinions towards aspects of the education system. This may produce references to forms of cultural capital that the research team had not previously considered.

e An excellent detailed knowledge of unstructured interviews is demonstrated in this paragraph and the candidate sees the need to use cultural capital as a means of illustrating his/her understanding. This is done reasonably well.

The objective of such interviews is to allow the interviewee to respond freely and in depth. Trust and rapport can be developed because the respondent can see that his or her input is valued and this may generate more qualitative and valid information about the respondent's interpretation of the world. The researcher does not end up imposing their view of cultural capital on the research subjects. Rather the trust generated by these interviews may lead to the interviewee telling the researcher information about their cultural capital that would not have been gained through a questionnaire or structured interview because it had previously been regarded as private and confidential.

e Excellent knowledge and understanding of unstructured interviews is demonstrated within the context of cultural capital.

In contrast, structured interviews are highly regarded by positivist sociologists who regard them as an important survey instrument. The structured interview is essentially a questionnaire of fixed questions which is read out to respondents and the answer recorded by the interviewer. Positivists are keen on structured interviews because they are thought to be highly reliable in that they are easily repeated by other sociologists and therefore data can be verified by others. Furthermore, such interviews are normally conducted with larger and more geographically scattered representative samples than research which uses unstructured interviews, therefore allowing generalisations to be made about particular populations and their experience of cultural capital. Finally, structured interviews are designed to generate quantitative data that can be easily converted into tables, graphs etc.

that can be compared and observed for trends and patterns. This allows sociologists to establish cause and effect relationships. For example, if cultural capital is operationalised effectively by the interview schedule, the statistical data may confirm relationships between social class and cultural capital.

e The candidate contrasts structured interviews with unstructured interviews by taking a theoretical approach. This is convincingly done — the candidate clearly links positivism to a scientific approach and intelligently discusses the elements of scientific research — reliability, representativeness, generalisability, quantifiability and cause/effect relationships.

However, the use of interviews can be criticised. Interpretivists argue that structured interviews suffer from the fact that they are essentially questionnaires and we can never be quite sure that the questions are understood in the same way by all those who are interviewed, although the sample could ask the interviewer for clarification. We have to assume that all possible facets of cultural capital have been covered by the questionnaire. However, any questionnaire reflects the sociologist's ideas and view of the world. It may be that the sociologist's experience of cultural capital may be very different to that of the subject, and consequently the interview schedule may fail to capture the subject's experience therefore reducing validity.

e This paragraph is an excellent assessment of structured interviews from a theoretical perspective.

In contrast, unstructured interviews are criticised by positivist sociologists for their lack of reliability. It is almost impossible to verify the interviewer's findings because another researcher would it find it impossible to replicate the quality of the relationship between the original interviewer and interviewee. There is also the danger that the relationship between the interviewer and interviewee may be biased because the interviewer unconsciously leads the interviewee into giving particular answers and/or the interviewee may want to please the interviewer by giving him/her what he/she wants. This social desirability effect which sometimes takes the form of 'yea-saying' may give a distorted and invalid picture of cultural capital. However, most sociologists would accept that the unstructured interview is less likely than the structured interview to experience these problems because interpretivist sociologists are more likely than positivist sociologist to reflect on the research process and assess their own influence on the research.

e The candidate shows great awareness of the pitfalls of unstructured interviews from a positivist point of view and intelligently attempts to show how interpretivist interviews practice reflexivity.

Overall, this response demonstrates both a detailed and focused theoretical and practical account of the strengths and weaknesses of the two types of interview. The candidate would score 5/5 for knowledge and understanding because it is very

apparent that this candidate has a excellent depth of understanding with regard to both the theoretical approaches and practicalities of interview research. The candidate would also score 4/5 for interpretation and analysis because he/she attempts to apply the concept of cultural capital throughout although this loses momentum in the latter stages. Finally, the candidate would be awarded 14/15 for an excellently constructed comparative analysis and evaluative assessment — the only shortcoming of which was the slightly inconsistent application of the concept of cultural capital. The candidate therefore would score an overall total of 23 marks out of a possible 25 — a clear grade-A response.

Answer to Option 1, question 3(a): grade-A candidate

Outline the evidence that challenges the view that 'we are all middle class now'.

The view that we are all middle class now was expressed by Tony Blair a few years ago. However, the evidence does not support Blair's view. If it did, it would show that people from all social backgrounds were experiencing similar standards of living and opportunities. This is not the case. The evidence quite clearly challenges Blair's view and shows that class differences are still as acute as they were 50 years ago and that poverty in the UK is a major problem.

e This is a good introduction which sets the scene for examining the evidence.

Income and wealth statistics are a good place to start. Fifty years ago, there were great inequalities in the distribution of wealth and income across social groups in the UK. The top 1% of the population owned over 40% of wealth in 1950. If we look at their share today, we can see a marked decline. They only owned about 18% in 2000. This is still a substantial inequality. In fact, we can see that what the wealthy seem to have done over the years is to transfer their wealth to other family members via trust funds. For example, in 2000, the top 10% of the wealthy owned nearly half of all wealth in the UK. This is hardly evidence of equality. Similarly, Will Hutton points out that in terms of income, the top 10% have actually got richer in the past 20 years while the bottom 10% have actually got poorer.

e There is excellent use of wealth and income statistics and the study by Hutton, but the candidate now needs to demonstrate wider sociological knowledge.

Another area of social life which indicates that class inequalities are actually growing is health. There is no doubt that for all sections of the population health has got better in that life expectancy has increased and all people are less likely to die of a range of diseases. However, the gap between middle-class and working-class life expectancy has widened. Members of the working class are living longer but not as long as those of the middle class. Moreover, the numbers of middle-class people surviving cancer and heart disease has increased at a much faster pace than the number of working-class people surviving such diseases.

Some relevant trends are highlighted and these count as evidence, but the candidate needs to focus on sociological studies as well in order to pick up all potential marks.

Wilkinson notes that middle-class people are more aware of health as an issue and are willing to seek advice from doctors in order to keep fit and healthy. They are more likely to take up active sports such as squash, tennis and golf. They also eat more healthily and think more about having a nutritious and fat-free diet. They are less likely to smoke and drink to excess too. Working-class people, on the other hand, are less likely to take an interest in how their lifestyle may be impacting upon their health. They are less likely to visit doctors for check-ups and more likely to indulge in fatty diets, especially those revolving around fast food. However, Wilkinson concludes that poor health has more to do with inequalities in income and wealth than cultural differences in behaviour.

This is an excellent section that identifies a good range of class-based differences in behaviour that may affect health, and uses the study of Wilkinson to explore some class-based explanations.

We can see that class is important in terms of the quality of family life and how it impacts upon education and achievement. For example, it is a fact that middle-class children achieve higher levels of education than working-class children. Evidence from studies of the middle class, e.g. by Savage, and studies of middle-class girls in private education, e.g. by Deborah Roker, indicate that middle-class children take for granted that they will go on to university and achieve professional and managerial occupational roles. These aspirations are generally absent from working-class children, who come from families with no experience of further and higher education. A recent study of poverty by the Joseph Rowntree Foundation found that children brought up in poverty had very low aspirations in terms of their education. The notion of taking A-levels and going to university was alien to them.

This is another excellent and perceptive section which at first seems as if it might be over-reliant on theory but compensates well by focusing on evidence from Savage, Roker and the Joseph Rowntree Foundation.

Overall, this candidate has demonstrated a wide-ranging knowledge of class differences and has very intelligently challenged the notion that the UK is a classless society. The candidate focuses on evidence throughout and understands this debate well. Most importantly, the response is synoptic, drawing on evidence from Inequality and Difference as well as education, family, health and community. Consequently, the candidate would be awarded 15/15 for knowledge and understanding of the evidence — the use of statistics and studies is excellent. 5/5 would be awarded for interpretation and application because the candidate is extremely focused on answering the question and is not attempting to explain why this evidence has come about or to evaluate it, which would be going beyond the remit of the question. Overall, the candidate would score 20 marks out of 20.

Answer to Option 1, question 3(b): grade-A candidate

Assess sociological explanations of the view that the changing nature of employment is having significant effects on class boundaries.

The nature of work in the UK has undergone great change in the past 30 years. In particular, the primary and secondary sectors of the economy have gone into decline. Heavy industries such as coal-mining and manufacturing or factory work have experienced recession because raw materials can be extracted and goods such as cars manufactured more cheaply in other parts of the world. Male manual work has consequently gone into decline.

e The candidate has decided, quite rightly, to focus on the changes to employment before focusing on their effects upon class boundaries.

However, we can also see that the tertiary or service sector of the economy — those jobs organised around the public sector (education, welfare etc.), personal services (such as retail) and finance — has expanded dramatically. The expansion of mass education, and especially the increase in people going into higher education, has meant that a well-educated and qualified workforce is available to take on these jobs. Many of the jobs available in this sector have been for women, especially in part-time work.

e The candidate contrasts the decline of the traditional sectors of work with the rise of the service sector and notes the feminisation of the labour force, although this is qualified with the reference to part-time work.

It is argued by postmodernist sociologists that assembly line production in factories, i.e. fragmented, simple, routine and boring tasks characterised by deskilling and controlled by a hierarchical management, have been replaced by robot technology and computers. However, it is also noted that work is no longer characterised by the stability of long-term security in the form of full-time contracts. Work today is likely to take the form of contracting out, to be temporary or part-time, and even casual.

e The candidate contrasts the nature of work in the industrial age with the nature of work today successfully, and begins to touch upon the implications for the class structure.

However, Marxists argue that manufacturing still makes up a major part of the economy and manual work still takes up a substantial part of the labour force. Moreover, the growth in the service sector has been long-standing — it is not a recent event and consequently employment in that sector has always been important. Marxists argue that new ways of organising factories are merely new ways of exploiting the labour force.

e There is some sustained and pertinent evaluation here, which implies that as far as the class structure is concerned little has changed.

So what has changed? There are a number of trends that we can be reasonably sure of. First, the process of deskilling and automation continues. In fact, some Marxists, particularly Braverman, argue that routine white-collar workers are no longer members of the middle class because employers are increasingly using technology, especially computers, to break down complex white-collar skills such as bookkeeping into simple routine tasks, in an attempt to increase output, maximise efficiency and reduce costs. These developments have been accompanied by the parallel development of feminising the white-collar workforce, because female workers are cheaper than male employees and are seen by employers to be more adaptable and flexible. Braverman concludes that white-collar workers have therefore been subjected to a process he calls 'proletarianisation', i.e. they have lost the social and economic advantages that they traditionally enjoyed over manual workers. He argues that they now have similar conditions of work and pay to blue-collar workers. A good example of this type of deskilling is the growth of call centres, which are not dissimilar in their workplace characteristics from factory assembly lines. White-collar workers in call centres are strictly controlled by management, have to take a set number of calls a day and keep to strict rules in the way they take those calls, and are allowed to take toilet and lunch breaks only at times set by management.

e This is a good section focusing on deskilling and proletarianisation, which uses the example of call centres well to illustrate the Marxist case. The consequences for class boundaries are very clearly laid out.

However, research by Devine suggests that Braverman may have overstated the case for proletarianisation, because her research indicates that distinct cultural differences in terms of values, lifestyles and political attitudes still exist between manual workers and white-collar workers. Moreover, white-collar workers still enjoy advantages over manual workers in terms of working conditions. They have access to flexitime, fringe benefits, longer holidays and safer working conditions.

e This is a very good evaluation of the Braverman argument.

Despite our scepticism in regard to proletarianisation, it can be safely assumed that deskilling is an ongoing process although its impact may have been exaggerated by some sociologists. There is evidence too in all sectors of work that the number of full-time workers on permanent contracts is on the decline. Instead, the economy is experiencing a casualisation of labour, i.e. more people are being hired on temporary contracts for shorter periods of time with few employment rights. In recent years, the recession has led to the downsizing of the financial sector and many managers have lost their jobs.

e This section is attempting to identify trends in regard to the changing nature of employment which might be impacting on class boundaries. This is quite a difficult task but the candidate has been reasonably successful.

There are a number of implications for class resulting from the above trends. Will Hutton argues that the traditional class categories (i.e. the Registrar-General's five-class categorisation) are now a little dated in the light of these changes. He argues that society is now split into a 30–30–40 society in that 30% of people are disadvantaged because they are unemployed and in poverty, 30% are marginalised and insecure because they are employed temporarily either part-time or casually, and 40% are privileged by having full-time, reasonably secure jobs.

e This is an excellent use of Hutton to illustrate the changing nature of employment and its effect upon social categories.

Even the authorities that define and measure class have adopted a new type of class categorisation to reflect these changes. The NS–SEC system of classifying occupations now takes into account people's employment relations, e.g. whether they work full-time or part-time, and market conditions, e.g. their salaries, promotion prospects and the degree of control they exercise over their work. This scale of occupations no longer divides workers along manual and non-manual lines.

e There is good use of the new social class scales to illustrate the changing nature of work.

Despite these changes to the nature of work, there are sociologists who argue that very little has changed in terms of class boundaries. Sociologists like Savage argue that non-manual workers have become the majority occupational group in the workforce (at 67%). He notes that most of the groups or class fractions that make up this group still continue to enjoy considerable material and cultural advantages over other occupational groups. Professionals, in particular, have consolidated their class position, and through home life and cultural capital are able to pass on their advantages to their children. Savage does acknowledge that three middle-class fractions have experienced some insecurity in recent years — the self-employed, managers and white-collar workers — but all continue, as Devine notes, to enjoy greater life chances than the working class.

e The candidate examines the other side of the coin, i.e. the view that there has been little change.

Marxists too, despite Braverman's thesis, argue that the position of the working class has hardly changed. The changes described above — deskilling, casualisation etc. — are merely part of the ongoing exploitative nature of capitalism and are likely to drive the working class closer still to poverty and revolutionary class consciousness. Critics, such as feminists, however, argue that Marxists are ignoring the crisis of masculinity that has been created by the fact that male jobs are being increasingly replaced by jobs for females. Some sociologists argue that this is the real problem created by the changing nature of work, because it is resulting in a mass of disaffected and alienated boys and men characterised by lack of qualifications and the potential for crime, urban disorder and violence against women.

The candidate ends with a brief discussion of the traditional Marxist view and a critique focusing perceptively on the crisis in masculinity.

Overall, this is a very good response. It identifies a range of possible changes in the way work is organised and shows a wide-ranging and detailed knowledge and understanding of the implications for class-boundary debates. This is an extremely wide debate and it is probably best to focus on some aspects of it in detail rather than try to deal with all aspects in a superficial fashion. This candidate does just this by deciding to focus on proleterianisation, the work of Hutton and the NS–SEC, although the concept of 'embourgeoisement' required some discussion. This candidate would score 13/15 for knowledge and understanding; 5/5 for interpretation and application and 17/20 for evaluation. The absence of any reference to the embourgeoisement argument meant that this candidate would not be awarded the full marks although the essay in general deserved the A grade that would be generated by 35 marks out of a possible 40.

Answer to Option 2, question 4(a): grade-A candidate

Outline the evidence that social class inequalities exist in the contemporary UK.

With regard to class inequalities, we can see that the evidence overwhelmingly supports the view that inequality is increasing in the contemporary UK. Statistics clearly show that between 1979 and 1997 income inequality between the rich and poor in Britain widened until it was at its most unequal since records began at the end of the nineteenth century. Average income rose by 36% during this period but the top 10% of earners experienced a 62% rise whilst the poorest 10% of earners experienced a 17% decline. In 2000, those in the service class earned well above the average national wage. In contrast, the Low Pay Unit estimated in 2000 that 45% of British workers were earning less than two-thirds of the average wage. In 2002–03, the richest 10% of the population received 29% of total disposable income (compared with 21% in 1979) whilst the poorest 10% received only 3% (compared with 4% in 1979).

A good start, focusing on social class inequalities in income although references to the top 10% of earners or wealthy needed a brief link to the notion of an upper class or ruling class. The statistics used could be more recent.

Similar inequalities can be seen within the field of wealth. In 2005, official statistics indicated that the top 10% owned 50% of the nation's wealth and the wealth of the most affluent 200 individuals and families doubled. This polarisation of wealth in the UK had also been encouraged by a soaring stock market (i.e. investing in stocks and shares) and property values which as Savage notes 'have allowed those who were already wealthy to accumulate their wealth massively'. Furthermore, although about 17% of all people own shares, the richest 1% of the population still own 75% of all privately owned shares. Roberts notes that the proportion of the population with enough wealth that they do not have

to work for others is still less than 1%. He notes too that it is only the extremely wealthy who can expect to die with most of their wealth intact.

Good use of studies by Savage and Roberts to illustrate inequalities in wealth as well as fairly recent statistics. Again, there was a need to link 'the extremely wealthy' or the 'most affluent 200 individuals' more firmly to social class.

In general, health across the population has improved over the last 30 years but the rate of improvement has been much slower for the working class. Generally, the working class experience poorer mortality rates and morbidity rates than the middle classes. For example, more than 3,500 working-class babies would survive per year if the working-class infant mortality rate was reduced to middle-class levels. In other words, babies born to professional fathers have levels of infant mortality half that of babies born to unskilled manual fathers. If we examine death rates we can see that, between 1972 and 1997, death rates for professionals fell by 44% but fell by only 10% for the unskilled. Bartley et al. (1996) note that men in Social Class I (using the old RG scale) had only two-thirds the chance of dying before retirement between 1986 and 1989 compared with the male population as a whole. However, unskilled manual workers were twice as likely to die before middle-class men.

Excellent section on health. This paragraph uses statistical trends in a convincing fashion as well as the Bartley study. It is also synoptic in that health is not an Inequality and Difference topic.

Bottero notes that the lower your socioeconomic position, the greater your risk of low birthweight, infections, cancer, coronary heart disease, respiratory disease, stroke, accidents, nervous and mental illnesses. Furthermore poor people are more likely to live in areas in which there are more hazards such as traffic and pollution and high crime rates.

This is a genuinely synoptic paragraph which intelligently links social class to a range of inequalities — health, community and crime.

Working-class children perform much worse in education than all other social groups at all levels of the education system. For example, more working-class children leave school at the age of 16 with no qualifications than middle-class 16-year-olds, and although the number of working-class 18-year-olds entering university has increased, the number of middle-class undergraduates still far exceeds them. For example, Connor and Dewson (2001) found that only one in five young people from working-class backgrounds participated in higher education.

Intelligent and synoptic summary of some of the evidence relating to social class inequalities in educational achievement. A good use of an empirical study is demonstrated by the use of Connor and Dewson.

Alcock identifies a range of different forms of poverty and exclusion that the working class in the UK experience, including lack of access to good quality private housing, poor access to aspects of the welfare state such as health and welfare benefits, educational inequalities, lack of political representation, being the victims of negative media stereotyping and over-zealous policing and physical harm and, in the case of black working-class people, fear from racist attacks.

The candidate finishes with a truly synoptic study that makes a range of relevant references to poverty, the welfare state, media representations, racism and politics. The choice of this study to finish the question was very intelligent because it hits so many targets.

Overall, this is an excellent response. This candidate would score 14/15 for knowledge and understanding of class inequality. Knowledge is detailed and clearly understood. The candidate resists the temptation to evaluate the information. 5/5 would be scored for interpretation and application because the candidate demonstrated a very good synoptic sensibility, i.e. he or she saw the need to apply a range of material and sources to the concept of class inequality. Overall, this candidate would achieve 19 marks out of a possible 20 — a grade-A response.

Answer to Option 2, question 4(b): grade-A candidate

Assess Marxist theories of stratification.

According to Karl Marx, capitalist society is characterised by a fundamental conflict between a rich, powerful minority (the bourgeoisie) and a powerless poor majority who survive only by working for the rich and powerful. Marx argued that the mode of production in capitalist societies is the manufacture of industrial goods in factories. He notes that the means of production — the resources required to manufacture, such as capital, land, factories, machinery and raw materials — are owned by the capitalist class.

An excellent introduction. This candidate gets straight to the point of the Marxist theory of stratification and understands that the theory must be outlined in some depth and detail before it can be assessed, i.e. before you can knock something down, you must build it up in the first place.

Marx also highlighted what he called the social relations of production — the way in which people are organised to produce things. He argued that these relations were characterised by an unequal and exploitative relationship between the capitalist class and the working class or proletariat.

According to Marx, the capitalist class relentlessly pursues profit and wealth and this involves a number of different types of exploitation. First, wages are kept as low as possible. Second, the bourgeoisie pocket the difference between what they pay their workers and the value of the goods produced by workers. This 'surplus value' forms the basis of their great wealth. Third, workers lose control over their jobs as new technology is introduced in order to increase output and therefore profits. Fourth, globalisation has meant that some sections of the capitalist class have relocated their factories abroad because labour costs in the developing world are cheaper, therefore making thousands of British workers redundant.

This paragraph demonstrates a sophisticated knowledge and understanding of a fairly complex concept — the social relations of production. Four points of illustration clearly show that this candidate is in control of the material.

However, Marx argued that workers are alienated by the social relations of production. They no longer enjoy work — it is merely a means to an end, i.e. money. However, Marx noted that workers rarely see themselves as exploited, because they have been 'duped' by ideological apparatuses such as education and the media into believing that capitalism is fair and natural. In his view, the working class were 'suffering' from a form of collective brainwashing known as false class-consciousness.

The candidate continues to demonstrate a good grasp of concepts — alienation, ideological apparatuses and false class consciousness are accurately discussed.

Marx believed that the conflict inherent in the capitalist system would eventually come to a head because the increasing concentration of wealth would cause the gap between rich and poor to grow, i.e. to become polarised, and consequently even the most short-sighted members of the proletariat would see that the time for change had come. Marx predicted that eventually the proletariat would unite, overthrow the bourgeoisie, seize the means of production for themselves and establish a fairer, more equal society known as Communism. For Marx, then, radical social change was inevitable as the working class was transformed from a class-in-itself into a revolutionary class-for-itself.

This is an excellent and insightful summary of Marx's predictions.

Marx's ideas had a huge influence in the twentieth century. Communist revolutions occurred in many countries such as China and Russia and it could be argued that his ideas have had more impact on more people than have the teachings of Jesus Christ and Mohammed put together. However, his ideas have come in for a great deal of criticism, especially since the communist regimes of Eastern Europe crumbled in the 1990s.

First, Marx is accused of being an economic determinist or reductionist, in that all his major ideas are based on the economic relationship between the bourgeoisie and proletariat. However, many contemporary conflicts, such as those rooted in nationalism, ethnicity and gender, cannot be explained adequately in economic terms.

We now see the candidate preparing the assessment. It is an excellent idea to begin with the strength of Marx's arguments in terms of their influence. The candidate balances this with the criticism of Marx as an economic determinist.

Second, Marx is criticised for underestimating the importance of the middle classes. He did recognise a third (in his view, relatively minor) class made up of professional workers, shopkeepers and clerks that he called the petit-bourgeoisie. However, being outside the system of production, they were deemed unimportant to the class struggle. In his view, as the two major camps polarised, members of this class would re-align their interests accordingly with either one. Some neo-Marxists have argued that the upper middle class have aligned themselves with the bourgeoisie, in that they act as agents for that class in their role of managers and professionals, i.e. the service class 'service' their employers. Others, most notably Braverman, argue that white-collar workers have more in common in terms of their working conditions with the proletariat.

This is an intelligent paragraph because it not only summarises Marx's ideas about the middle class but it is also willing to explore neo-Marxist perspectives on this class, which it does lucidly and convincingly.

Third, Marx's prediction that the working class would become 'class conscious' because they would experience extreme misery and poverty, and therefore seek to transform the capitalist system, has not occurred. Working-class people in the UK do have a sense of class identity but this is limited. Surveys suggest that most people who see themselves as working class do so not because they recognise their exploited status but because they wish to claim their typicality in terms of being working people. Furthermore, although Western capitalist societies may have problems such as poverty and homelessness, they do have a reasonably good record in terms of democracy and workers' rights. Moreover, the living standards of the working class have risen. It may be then that working-class people are sensibly reconciled to capitalism rather than being 'falsely conscious'. In other words, they appreciate the benefits of capitalism despite being aware of the inequalities generated by it.

This is perceptive evaluation which challenges the concept of false class consciousness in an articulate and contemporary fashion.

Neo-Marxists have tended to focus on the relationship between the infrastructure, i.e. the capitalist economy and particularly the social relationships of production characterised by class inequality, exploitation and subordination, and the superstructure (i.e. all the major social institutions of society, e.g. education, the mass media, religion, the law, the political system etc.). Neo-Marxists argue that the function of the superstructure is the reproduction and legitimation of the class inequality found in the infrastructure. In other words, the superstructure exists to transmit ruling class ideology and, in particular, to make sure that the mass of society subscribes to ruling class ideas about how society should be organised. It does not complain too much about the inequality, for example in income and wealth, that exists. The function of the superstructure, therefore, is to encourage acceptance of class stratification and to ensure that false class-consciousness continues among the working class.

The candidate rightly sees the need to extend the debate beyond the work of Marx. The distinction and relationship between the infrastructure and superstructure is handled well.

Education is seen by neo-Marxists as a particularly important ideological apparatus working on behalf of the capitalist class. Marxists such as Althusser suggest that education transmits the idea that society is a meritocracy, i.e. that ability is the major mechanism of success, but this disguises the reality of the stratification system, i.e. that those born into ruling or middle-class backgrounds are much more likely to achieve because wealth, private education and an 'old boys' network' opens the doors to Oxbridge and makes it easier for the children of these classes to achieve top jobs, compared with the children of the working class.

The candidate summarises the ideas of Althusser well. Bourdieu's ideas about cultural capital might have been introduced here too.

Other neo-Marxists have focused on the ideological power of the mass media and how the bourgeoisie might be using this to their advantage. The Frankfurt School of Marxists, for example, writing since the 1930s, have focused on the role of the media in creating a popular culture for the masses that has diverted working-class attention away from the unequal nature of capitalism to an obsession with materialism, celebrity culture and trivia. Marcuse, for example, noted that capitalism has been successful in persuading the working class that their priorities lie with consumerism rather than revolution or dissent. Neo-Marxists argue that people are deliberately kept ignorant by the modern media and, consequently, stratification and class inequality in terms of wealth, income and monarchy are rarely challenged.

This paragraph demonstrates a good understanding of ideology — the candidate applies the concept in an insightful manner to the mass media.

Saunders (1990) criticises Marxist writers because they claim to know a truth which is hidden from others. Saunders claims this is a form of intellectual arrogance. It suggests that Marxists know the truth because Marxist theory is true. In addition, Marxist theory dismisses what working-class people say and think about their situation as the product of ideology and consequently false class-consciousness. However, working-class people may be aware of inequality but may see it as an unfortunate by-product of a system which actually benefits the majority of workers.

This candidate has remembered that the neo-Marxist version requires assessment. The evaluation is an intelligent and incisive dissection of ideology and false class-consciousness.

Max Weber (1947) rejected the Marxist emphasis on social class as the sole cause of inequality in modern capitalist society. Weber saw 'class' and 'status' as two separate but related sources of power that have overlapping effects on people's life chances. Weber argued that status did not come exclusively from class — he noted that status differences can originate in gender, ethnic, religious and power differences too. However, he did see class as the most important of these three interlinking factors.

It was important to contrast Marxism with another theory. Weber is probably best suited to this although the functionalists Davis and Moore could have been used instead.

The Marxist theory of stratification has made a great contribution to our understanding of modern capitalist societies. Although it does have some problems, e.g. Marx's predictions have not come true, there is no denying that social class inequalities in terms of wealth, income, health, education etc. are an important consequence of the way capitalism is organised in the UK. Even Weber agreed that social class was the major source of inequality in capitalist societies.

Many students forget to write a conclusion and although this one is not brilliant, it quickly summarises the Marxist view that social class creates inequality. It is a reasonably succinct and focused ending to an excellent essay.

Overall, this candidate knows the Marxist theory of stratification very well and has produced an essay which shows an outstanding understanding of Marxist concepts and ideas. The outlining of the theory is conducted with depth of detail, and it is obvious that the candidate has a good deal of confidence. The evaluation, too, is managed convincingly. It is not content to just look at the weaknesses but it also makes a brief attempt to assess strengths. In terms of knowledge and understanding, the candidate is awarded 15/15, and the organisational skills exhibited attract 5/5 for interpretation and application. The evaluation is excellent but might have included reference to alternative arguments such as functionalism or feminism, in addition to Weber. However, this is a minor criticism and the candidate is awarded 17/20 marks. Overall, the candidate scores 37/40.

Ethnic minority women and work

Read Item B and answer questions 1 and 2, and then answer either Option 1, 3(a) and 3(b) or Option 2, 4(a) and 4(b).

Item B

The overall aim of this investigation was to understand more about the diverse experiences and aspirations of ethnic minority women in relation to work, including barriers to progress, so that effective action could be taken to improve their labour market prospects. The investigation focused particularly on Bangladeshi, Pakistani and black Caribbean women. Pakistani and Bangladeshi women were included because they have the lowest rates of employment of any other ethnic group, and black Caribbean women because they are under-represented in senior level jobs.

The research design was multi-levelled. It involved:

- pilot interviews with 22 experts and managers who had substantial experience of equality and diversity issues
- 11 focus group interviews covering 43 women in London, Birmingham and Bristol aimed at exploring the experiences of women in varied circumstances
- six case studies of organisations which employed ethnic minority women; in each case study organisation, face-to-face in-depth interviews were carried out with ten women employees (a mix of Bangladeshi, black Caribbean and Pakistani) and two managers
- documents pertaining to the organisation and its policies were collected

Women who owned small businesses or worked within ethnically owned businesses were interviewed.

Altogether 152 people took part in the study, of which 130 were ethnic minority women.

The research revealed that 54% of black Caribbean women often had difficulty finding work (compared with only 34% of white women). It also found that increasingly black women are forced to take jobs below their skills and experience levels. Almost one-third (31%) of black Caribbean women had seen less experienced or less qualified people promoted above them, and a third had experienced racist comments at work. Pakistani and Bangladeshi women have low economic activity rates, high unemployment rates and are more heavily concentrated than white women in a 'restricted' range of occupations (including retail, clerical work and educational support work). The study therefore

> concluded that despite a skill shortage, there is an under-utilisation of existing talent with regard to ethnic minority women. Caribbean women are clustered in the public sector, frequently in lower level occupations than their experience or qualifications merit. Talent is therefore lost from an organisation if women leave because they feel they have been overlooked for promotion, especially when they see less-qualified white men and women progressing more quickly.
>
> Bradley, H., Healy, G., Forson, C. and Kaul, P. (2007) *Workplace cultures: what does and does not work*, Equal Opportunities Commission

Compulsory questions

1 **Using the item and your own knowledge outline and explain why some sociologists claim focus group interviews produce data that lack validity.** (15 marks)

2 **Outline and assess the reliability of case studies in producing valid data about ethnic minority women's experience of the workplace.** (25 marks)

Then answer either:

Option 1

3 (a) **Outline the evidence for the view that racism is a common experience in UK society.** (20 marks)

(b) **Assess Marxist explanations of why some ethnic minorities experience inequality in the workplace.** (40 marks)

OR

Option 2

4 (a) **Outline the evidence for the view that patriarchy remains a feature of most aspects of UK society.** (20 marks)

(b) **Assess sociological explanations of gender inequality in the workplace.** (40 marks)

Answer to compulsory question 1: grade-A candidate

Using the item and your own knowledge outline and explain why some sociologists claim focus group interviews produce data that lack validity.

Focus group interviews are a fairly modern invention with regards to social science. They have been used in political science and advertising for many years but it is only in the past 10 years that they have been used in sociological research. For example, many media sociologists have used focus group interviews to explore how audiences interpret media content.

e This is a brief but very good introduction to focus group interviews which contextualises the contemporary nature of the method.

Focus group interviews involve getting a group of people together and exposing them to particular stimuli — this might be made up of images, adverts or even statements — and then allowing them to discuss amongst themselves the meaning or impact of that stimuli upon their and others' lives. The sociologist normally plays two roles. First, the researcher will observe the group's interactions, body language etc. when discussing the subject matter. Often they will be filmed and recorded. Second, the researcher will act as a manager or facilitator by injecting the discussion with questions if it starts to falter and chairing the discussion to make sure that it stays on track and is sufficiently detailed. The focus group interview is therefore a type of unstructured interview in that it is not controlled by a rigid questionnaire, members of the group are encouraged to explore their feelings, attitudes etc. in depth and consequently qualitative data which are expressed in the focus group's own words and which therefore are high in validity are produced. Consequently, focus group interviews have especially appealed to interpretivist sociologists.

e **This is an excellent summary of how focus groups work in principle. There is a brief but relevant link to theory.**

The source suggests that the 11 focus group interviews covering 43 ethnic minority women from different cities across the UK will gather qualitative evidence relating to their experience and interpretations of racial prejudice and discrimination in the workplace.

e **The candidate remembers to use the source material. It is often tempting under examination conditions for candidates to merely copy material from the source material but this candidate has attempted to reword it and implicitly linked it to the interpretivist approach.**

However, positivist sociologists would probably criticise the design and organisation of focus group interviews as unscientific for a number of reasons. First, they believe that research should be carried out under controlled conditions. They would probably argue that focus group interviews are uncontrollable because strong personalities may dominate discussion. Other members of the group may be too shy and retiring to make a contribution, therefore, all points of view may not be truly represented which make the results difficult to generalise to the research population.

e **The evaluation is theoretically contextualised in a convincing fashion.**

Second, positivists would suggest that focus group interviews are unreliable because it is almost impossible to replicate the interaction that takes place within them. It is therefore impossible to verify the results gathered. Positivists would also be concerned about the objectivity of such research. A fantastic amount of data are collected by such methods and there is a danger that material may be selected that suits the hypothesis, and any conflicting evidence may be neglected or ignored.

The candidate clearly outlines and intelligently illustrates problems relating to reliability and objectivity.

Another potential problem may result from the type of data that are collected. Positivists prefer quantitative data that can be converted into graphs, tables etc. and be observed for correlations in order to establish social laws about human behaviour. Focus group interviews, on the other hand, probably generate qualitative data, i.e. verbatim discussions and quotations, which are difficult to compare or analyse. The study in the source material, however, aims to overcome these problems by using other methods such as interviewing managers and experts, looking at secondary data such as documents and by carrying out case studies of organisations that employ black women.

An excellent paragraph which not only identifies a possible weakness of focus groups but clearly describes how the study in the source material will overcome these potential problems.

Interpretivist sociologists are very keen on focus group interviews because such research focuses on the meanings that people use to make sense of the social world. They argue that it is important to investigate how the social world looks from the point of view or interpretations of those being studied. If facilitators are skilled at group management, trust and rapport should be achieved in a secure and comfortable environment which produces valid data. They therefore would argue that focus group interviews are high in validity because they produce qualitative data which speaks in the words of the participants themselves and reflects the meanings that people attach to their everyday experiences.

An excellent and insightful paragraph linking focus groups very confidently to the interpretivist tradition.

Generally this is an excellent response from a candidate who has an excellent stock of knowledge about focus groups and is able to apply that understanding very intelligently to the research design mentioned in the source material. This candidate would therefore score 10/10 for knowledge and understanding and 5/5 for interpretation and application, therefore securing the full mark of 20 out of 20.

Answer to compulsory question 2: grade-A candidate

Outline and assess the reliability of case studies in producing valid data about ethnic minority women's experience of the workplace.

A case study is a sociological research technique which involves an in-depth study of a single example of whatever the sociologist is interested in. The example studied might be an individual (e.g. a criminal or delinquent), group (e.g. a gang or ethnic minority female workers), organisation (e.g. a company that employs ethnic minority women), community (e.g. a village), nation or event (e.g. a riot). Usually a case study will involve the sociologist using a variety of primary and secondary research

methods, i.e. methodological pluralism, in order to build up a multifaceted picture of the research subject gained from a number of different angles.

A detailed, fulsome definition and description of the case study is offered by this paragraph. This candidate is not just content to describe but he/she positively shows off his/her understanding by the consistent use of illustrative examples.

With an organisational case study, the sociologist might study a factory, office or company with the aim of getting inside the 'life' of the institution in question using methodological pluralism in order to see how different groups such as ethnic minority women experience the institution. For example, for a case study of a factory, the sociologist might interview the shop-floor workers in order to find out about their levels of perceived racism and being overlooked for promotion. The sociologist might use participant observation to look at the daily experience of black women as well as issuing a questionnaire to a sample of ethnic minority employees at all levels of the organisation in order to establish whether they feel they are being discriminated against. Interviews might also be carried out with white managers to see whether their perception of relations with ethnic minority employees is similar to that of those employees. Secondary data might be taken from equal opportunity statistics regarding the numbers of black people at work at particular levels and compared with the case study company. Once all of these data were analysed and interpreted, the sociologist would have a comprehensive insight into the experience of ethnic minorities at work.

This is a detailed attempt to practically apply the method of case study to the study of ethnic minority women in the workplace. It is very successful in its design and understanding.

The other type of case study involves in-depth analysis of the experiences and views of a small sample of individuals with similar experiences. For example, a sociologist might study a small group of individuals who had all been victims of racism at work in order to find out how respondents had altered their working habits as a result of their experiences. In order to carry out this research, the method of semi-structured interviews could be used. In addition, the case-study approach usually necessitates repeated interviews, over a period of time, which gives more depth and also the possibility of recording changes that occur in the respondent's life, attitudes, etc. In some circumstances, the sociologist would try to gain access to any personal documents, e.g. letters and diaries, that might give insight into the life experiences or life history of the respondents, or might ask people to keep diaries recording their fears about racism at work.

The practical application of case studies is developed further in an extremely perceptive fashion.

Interpretivists are very keen on case studies because they believe that sociological research should attempt to access the everyday lives of the research subjects and try to see the social world through their eyes so that their interpretation of social reality can be understood. Case studies often result in a high degree of insight into people's experiences. Moreover they offer respondents the opportunity to give an insight into their emotions and motives as well as their experiences. The case study stresses the viewpoints and interpretations of those being studied and therefore scores highly in terms of validity.

An excellent theoretical context is constructed by the candidate.

However, the case study approach may experience some difficulties. The organisation or group being studied may not be typical or representative of society as a whole, so generalisation from case studies may not be possible. Positivist sociologists point out that the reliability of data is sometimes questionable, especially when respondents are asked to remember past events.

This candidate evaluates case studies from a positivist perspective although the points made are a little superficial.

The emphasis therefore in the use of methodological pluralism in case studies is on building up a fuller and more comprehensive picture of social life by generating different types of data which shed light on different parts of the research problem. This differs from the classic form of triangulation which aims primarily to use one method in order to cross-check data from another. Methodological pluralism therefore has the advantage of the strength of one method compensating for or helping to overcome the limitations of another. There are few areas of social life where one research method alone is sufficient to gain a meaningful insight into people's lives.

This candidate has rightly recognised that case studies involve methodological pluralism. The approach is clearly defined and the strength of the method is intelligently outlined.

However, critics point out that the pluralist case study approach can be expensive. Moreover case studies produce vast amounts of data which can be difficult to compare and analyse. Sociologists using this approach are often accused of selectivity and ignoring those data that do not fit in with their values. For example, some ethnic minority women may report no experience of prejudice in the workplace but researchers may over-focus in their write-up of the results on those women who did experience it.

Another attempt at evaluation which is reasonably successful and which applies the criticism to the study in the source material.

Overall, this response shows a confident understanding of the concept of case studies and clearly contextualises the research method with regard to theory and methodological pluralism. However, its most impressive aspect is the willingness of the candidate to use detailed examples from the source material to illustrate the strengths and weaknesses of case studies throughout the response. This is generally very successful. Consequently, the candidate is awarded 5/5 marks for knowledge and

understanding and 5/5 for interpretation and application. Evaluation scored 13/15 because there was a little superficiality in the discussion of weaknesses. This candidate would therefore achieve 22 marks out of a possible 25.

Answer to Option 1, question 3(a): grade-A candidate

Outline the evidence for the view that racism is a common experience in UK society.

Racism is a term that covers a wide range of discriminatory practices and negative beliefs, attitudes and stereotypes, i.e. prejudice, which result in black people having poorer jobs, health, education, housing and life chances compared with the white majority.

e The candidate begins with a definition of the components of racism, although the answer needs to move on to examine the evidence as soon as possible.

Studies of racial prejudice in the UK suggest that a substantial minority of white people admit to being prejudiced against black people. For example, a European Union-wide survey conducted in 1997 found that one in three Britons (32%) believed themselves to be very racist (8%) or quite racist (24%).

e This is a good, reasonably contemporary example.

Studies of mass media content suggest a racist agenda, especially in the tabloid press. Content analysis studies, e.g. Van Dijk, suggest that black people are often stereotyped as a threat to white society in terms of immigration, crime, drugs, welfare dependency etc. It is believed that the media transmit racist myths and fears and, on occasion, create moral panics about ethnic minorities which reinforce prejudice and may even create the climate for racial harassment, name-calling and violence.

e The candidate is using wider sociological knowledge well to access synoptic material from AS study of the mass media.

There is evidence of employer discrimination against black people in terms of jobs. Brown surveyed over 5,000 black people and concluded that many of his sample had experienced discrimination in terms of job applications, but also from landlords, building societies, council housing departments etc. when searching for somewhere to live. Such discrimination probably explains why black people are found in disproportionate numbers in low-skilled manual work and privately rented accommodation.

e This paragraph is in danger of over-generalising the experience of black people. However, the Brown research is a good piece of evidence to cite and goes beyond the Social Inequality and Difference unit by focusing on housing.

The Home Office has recently highlighted the problem of racial attacks in our society, in the light of the Stephen Lawrence Inquiry. It is estimated by the government that, compared with white people, Asians are 50 times and

African-Caribbeans 36 times more likely to be victims of a racially motivated attack in the UK. Figures suggest 8,000 reported racial attacks in the UK every year, but this is likely to be an underestimate.

This is a good contemporary reference to the Stephen Lawrence Inquiry, and again there is evidence of wider sociological knowledge accessing material about crime and deviance.

There is some evidence of police racism. The Stephen Lawrence Inquiry accused the police of institutional racism. This is where racism is embedded, perhaps unconsciously, in the rules, regulations and everyday practices of an organisation. Studies of police forces and officers on the beat, e.g. Smith and Grey, and Holdaway, have indicated that some police officers do operate with negative stereotypes of black people, and assume that their behaviour is more suspicious or criminal than that of white people.

The candidate extends the debate to include 'institutional racism', which is defined clearly and linked to evidence regarding police behaviour.

Finally, some sociologists have accused the education system in the UK of institutional racism too. Wright's ethnographic study of four inner-city primary schools suggests that teachers exclude Asian children from group discussions because they assume they have a poor command of English, while the same teachers assume that African-Caribbean boys are disruptive and difficult to deal with. These negative views result in African-Caribbean boys being treated more harshly. Such children, argued Wright, develop low self-esteem or become hostile to the classroom and this may result in educational underachievement. Other studies, e.g. the Swann Report, have suggested that the knowledge taught in schools (the national curriculum) and teaching methods are ethnocentric — they reflect white rather than black experience and therefore 'turn off' black children from the learning process.

This is another excellent example of wider sociological knowledge. This section focuses clearly on evidence in its referencing of Wright and Swann.

Overall, the candidate demonstrates an excellent and perceptive wider sociological understanding, using material which is clearly focused on evidence relating to education, crime and deviance, housing, racial attacks, mass media representations, general prejudice and jobs. A response of this quality would score the full marks of 15 for knowledge and understanding and 5 marks for interpretation and application.

Answer to Option 2, question 4(a): grade-A candidate

Outline the evidence for the view that patriarchy remains a feature of most aspects of UK society.

The most obvious evidence that patriarchy remains a key feature of UK society is that relating to employment. Crompton and Le Feuvre (1996) argue that the most important factor determining whether a woman works or not is whether she has

children, and especially the age of the youngest child. Men are not subject to such influences. Whether women work part-time or take time out of the labour market (which negatively affects their long-term promotion prospects compared with men) depends largely on social expectations. Patriarchal ideology expects that women should be primarily concerned with domestic and especially childcare commitments. Hartnett notes that employers may unconsciously discriminate against women if they have children because of the patriarchal belief that women will put their children before their commitment to work.

e **This is a good start. The candidate focuses on how patriarchal beliefs or ideology shape our thinking and especially the thinking of employers about women, and how this results in women not enjoying the same life chances as men.**

The result of such patriarchal thinking is that men and women have segregated experiences of work. Women are much more likely than men to work part-time (women constitute 84% of all part-time workers) and on average women only earn about 80% of what men earn. Moreover, women experience horizontal segregation, i.e. women mainly work with other women in the fields of clerical, secretarial, sales and personal service work whereas men dominate engineering, mechanics and agriculture. Women also experience vertical segregation — they are less likely than men to be found in top professional and managerial jobs.

e **Good use of concepts is demonstrated in this section. The candidate identifies accurate evidence in the form of trends relating to vertical and horizontal segregation of work.**

In the family, evidence relating to the patriarchal nature of society can be seen in the distribution of male and female labour in the home. The work of Leonard suggests that a gender role ideology determines whether housework and childcare is shared between men and women. Leonard notes that women who subscribe to a patriarchal gender role ideology see housework and childcare as an essential part of being a 'good wife and mother' and rarely complain about the non-participation of their partner. Leonard's empirical research into domestic labour indicates that few men share such tasks. As Leonard concludes, this division of labour suits men because it means that they can resist change.

e **The candidate is using wider sociological knowledge to present evidence relating to gender roles within the family. Most candidates simply present statistical evidence of the inequality of domestic labour, but this candidate goes further by exploring research into the ideology of the home using the work of Madeleine Leonard.**

In education too, we can see the influence of patriarchal attitudes. Despite improvements in female performance in education, there is evidence of continued gendered choices in subjects, especially at the further and higher education levels. Ann Colley's research indicates that such gendered choices may be partly responsible for creating horizontal segregation in the types of jobs men and women go into. Mirza's research suggests that the careers service and some teachers play a crucial role in pushing males and females towards gendered careers, which reproduce patriarchal divisions in the labour market.

e Further and wider sociological knowledge relating to education is demonstrated here. The references to Colley and Mirza contextualise the response in terms of evidence.

There is also evidence suggesting gender divisions in mortality and morbidity. Women live longer than men (this also contributes to making female pensioners one group most at risk of poverty). However, evidence suggests that women record higher rates of illness than men, especially mental illness. Research by Hilary Graham points out that these higher rates of illness might be due to women bearing most of the responsibility for domestic labour and the physical and emotional care of their families, the dual burden of paid work and domestic labour, greater exposure to poverty etc. In fact, the research of Jesse Bernard led her to conclude that marriage makes women sick. According to Hicks, women face greater stress because they are likely to be caring for both children and other relatives such as ageing parents. There is some evidence that women may appear in the mental health statistics more than men because, as Busfield notes, male doctors are more likely to view certain types of behaviour as feminine and therefore unstable.

e This is a very good section which is focused explicitly on evidence relating to death and illness. The references to Graham, Bernard and Hicks are excellent, as are the references to mental illness. Overall, the candidate focuses convincingly on a wide range of both practical and theoretical evidence. This candidate would be awarded the full marks available for both knowledge and understanding, and interpretation and application.

Answer to Option 2, question 4(b): grade-A candidate

Assess sociological explanations of gender inequality in the workplace.

As we have already seen, there is considerable evidence of gender inequality in the workplace relating to the distribution of full-time and part-time jobs, pay, and vertical and horizontal segregation. Such inequalities are generally connected to other types of gender inequality, especially within the family or health and welfare provision. For example, women tend to take responsibility for domestic labour and family health (while according a low priority to their own). Their lack of continuous work experience may mean that they lack welfare rights such as pensions that men take for granted.

e A good introduction sets the scene of the debate by thinking about a range of possible inequalities.

Moreover, it is important to note that gender interacts with ethnicity because women from ethnic minority groups are much more likely than white women to face inequalities in the labour market.

e This is a good point which demonstrates that the candidate is thinking evaluatively.

Neo-Weberian accounts of gender inequality in the workplace have focused on the concepts of a dual labour market. Barron and Norris claim that two markets exist for labour: the primary sector, which is dominated by men and is made up of skilled well-paid jobs with long-term promotion paths clearly laid out; and the secondary labour market, which is dominated by women and ethnic minorities and is made up of unskilled, low-paid and insecure jobs. Hartnett argues that women are generally allocated to the secondary labour market because employers subscribe to patriarchal beliefs about women's commitment to their careers. Moreover, employers are supposedly less likely to invest in expensive training programmes for women who have not had children, believing that they are likely to interrupt their careers to have them. Caplow notes that child-rearing also interrupts the continuous service required for promotion. In addition, the legal framework supporting equal rights and pay in the UK, i.e. the Equal Opportunities Act and Equal Pay Act, is weakly enforced by the state. Consequently, this theory is sceptical that increased educational qualifications for females will make much difference to women's opportunities, because the glass ceiling is maintained by patriarchal ideology rather than women's lack of experience or ability.

This is an excellent paragraph which clearly and accurately explains the dual labour market theory.

However, Bradley is critical of Barron and Norris's theory because the evidence suggests that women can break into the primary sector, although it is unclear why women tend to occupy the bottom rungs of professional and managerial work.

Some specific evaluation is included but it requires further detail and development.

Feminist accounts of gender inequality at work vary, although all suggest that patriarchy — male domination of social structures, ideas and culture — plays a crucial role. For example, in the 1970s, liberal feminists like Oakley pointed to familistic ideology (Leonard calls it 'gender role ideology') which was influential in persuading both men and women that women's primary goal was the mother–housewife role. They would argue that such ideologies are still influential and can be seen in subject choice for females at the further and higher education levels.

This paragraph defines patriarchy succinctly and introduces its influence via 1970s liberal feminism, while acknowledging in an evaluative way that this theory may still be relevant today.

Marxist feminists insist that capitalism is responsible for gender inequalities in the workplace. Beechey argues that women form part of the 'reserve army of labour' which is essential to help capitalists manage the boom–bust nature of capitalism with minimum disruption and instability. Such a workforce is hired in times of economic expansion and fired in times of recession. However, capitalist ideology stresses that the 'natural' place for women is in the home, so therefore redundancy and unemployment for women provokes little protest from society.

Moreover, domestic labour is crucial because it reproduces and maintains the future and present workforces respectively. However, this Marxist analysis has been criticised because it does not explain why there are men's jobs and women's jobs. It does not explain why women who do succeed in professional and management jobs can get only so far. Finally, it suggests that women's labour is cheaper than men's — if this was the case, surely the capitalist class would replace male labour with cheaper female labour?

e This is another excellent summary with an evaluative commentary.

Some Marxists, such as Hartmann, have attempted to suggest that patriarchy and capitalism operate together to oppress women. Hartmann notes that low pay operates to keep women economically dependent upon men, which encourages marriage and domestic labour. This further benefits men by supporting their careers while further weakening women's position in the labour market because they are unavailable to take paid work.

e This is a good paragraph that makes synoptic links between work and family.

Walby has probably constructed the most convincing explanations of gender inequalities at work, using the triple systems approach. She notes that patriarchy has three elements to it: subordination or unequal relations between the sexes; oppression, i.e. discrimination; and exploitation, i.e. women gain little reward for their labour. Walby argues that the family is over-played as the major source of patriarchy. Rather she notes that many households (and therefore men in their roles as husbands or partners) depend upon women's participation in the labour force for financial stability. She therefore argues that the causes of women's inequality in the labour market are not the roles women play within the family. Instead she blames employers who have organised the workforce into full-time and part-time work in order to exploit all workers (not just women) more effectively and flexibly in response to the changing nature of work. Moreover, she points out that gender inequality is maintained by the state, which has been slow to respond to social change.

e Another excellent summary of a complex theory is given.

Finally, Hakim has been critical of feminist theories of workplace inequality. She claims that they neglect the fact that women are actively engaged in making rational choices about their futures. To put it simply, she argues that women are not as committed to work and careers as men because women give priority to marriage and childcare. She suggests that feminism has been allowed to devalue family life. Inequality in the workplace, therefore, is not caused by patriarchy but by intelligent women choosing to reject careers. Unsurprisingly, feminists have been unwilling to accept this position and Crompton, in particular, has pointed out that women do not make choices in a cultural vacuum. Rather, the choices women have are constrained by their lack of power and resources relative to those held by men. It could be argued that ethnic minority women are similarly constrained. They cannot make the same decisions about work and family as white women, as they may be constrained by culture, religion and racism.

e This is an excellent evaluative paragraph which covers Hakim's critique of feminism but also incorporates a feminist response to her ideas, plus an evaluative comment about women from ethnic minority backgrounds.

Overall, this is a high-quality response to the question. It covers a wide range of complex theoretical material clearly and accurately. It has an evaluative tone throughout and addresses the specifics of key issues in an analytical way. Although the candidate might have evaluated issues of social class (e.g. feminism assumes a universal gender experience at times and fails to distinguish between working-class and middle-class gendered experience) and ethnicity more deeply (some of the theories discussed take analysis of women and ethnicity a step further), this is still a first-class response. It would be awarded 13/15 for knowledge and understanding and 5/5 for interpretation and application. Evaluation was its weakest characteristics but it would still be placed in the top band of the marking scheme scoring 17/20 marks. Overall, this response would be awarded 35 marks out of a possible 40, a clear grade-A.

Vulnerable young men and employment

Read Item C and answer questions 1 and 2, and then answer either Option 1, 3(a) and 3(b) or Option 2, 4(a) and 4(b).

Item C

The main aim of this report was to provide a better understanding of the reasons why some young men are able to overcome the impact of a period of long-term unemployment at an early stage in their careers while others face a future of recurrent unemployment and precarious employment.

A total of 32 biographical interviews, each lasting around 90 minutes, were conducted with men aged 25 to 29 years in a range of urban and rural areas. In selecting the sample, the researchers ensured that those with extensive experience of unemployment were well represented. Many had multiple disadvantages (for example, residing in areas of high deprivation, coming from 'work-poor' families or having long-term health problems). The interviews were holistic in focus (covering labour market experiences from full-time employment to informal work, education, training, illegal activities, family, domestic and housing transitions) with the central concern being to identify the ways in which young men overcame the impact of long-term unemployment in their early careers or, conversely, the reasons why the impact of early experiences continued to affect their lives. The researchers also conducted interviews with 13 key officials who worked with young unemployed adults.

The study found that most of the young men who took part in the study were vulnerable workers. They had failed to thrive in a school environment for a number of reasons, and consequently, they tended to leave school at the earliest opportunity with few, if any, qualifications. Transitions from school to work were often turbulent and involved protracted (and usually repeated) periods of unemployment as well as time on schemes such as Youth Training. The majority of the sample were either in precarious forms of employment or were experiencing unemployment.

With most young men readily accepting any opportunity to work or train for new jobs, there was little evidence to suggest that the young men were feckless and preferred to live on benefits rather than work. The study also found that loss of self-confidence may prevent young people from applying for certain types of jobs, and lead to a downgrading of expectations. It can affect performance at interviews.

Furlong, A. and Cartmel, F. (2004) *Vulnerable young men in fragile labour markets: Employment, unemployment and the search for long-term security*, Joseph Rowntree Foundation

Compulsory questions

1 **Using the item and your own knowledge outline and explain how representative samples may be selected for surveys that aim to target young men across a range of urban and rural areas.** (15 marks)

2 **Outline and assess the reliability of biographical interviews in producing valid data about young men's experience of unemployment.** (25 marks)

Then answer either:

Option 1

3 (a) **Outline the evidence that suggests that some types of inequality are increasing in the contemporary UK.** (20 marks)

(b) **Assess functionalist explanations of social inequality.** (40 marks)

OR

Option 2

4 (a) **Outline the evidence that a young underclass exists in the UK.** (20 marks)

(b) **Assess sociological explanations of age inequality.** (40 marks)

Task

This paper is for you to try. You should spend some time researching suitable material and making notes, and then try to write the answer in 90 minutes — the time you will be allowed in the examination. Below are a few pointers to help you get on the right track.

Question 1

This question mainly demands knowledge and understanding on how surveys use random sampling techniques such as stratified sampling. You will need to begin by explaining why random sampling is deemed important by positivist sociologists. You should follow up by describing the different types that are available to sociologists but don't forget to discuss how the research design in the source material organises sampling and why.

Question 2

This question is mainly testing your evaluation skills. Outline what is meant by biographical interviews, e.g. are these structured or unstructured? Are they preferred by positivist or interpretivist sociologists? Don't forget to say how they might produce valid data about young men in employment, i.e. the aim of the study in the source material. Most importantly, what problems may undermine the validity of these interviews? You should focus in depth on interview bias or effect.

Questions 3 and 4

Whichever option you decide to go for, it is important that you think about the following. First, note that part (a) asks you to 'outline' evidence — this means describe it. There is no need to explain it or to evaluate it. Second, the part (a) questions stress evidence — this usually takes the form of statistics or trends, and sociological studies. The names of sociologists who have actually carried out research should be cited whenever possible. Third, these are synoptic questions so you must use evidence taken from other areas of the specification in addition to the Exploring Social Inequality and Difference material, e.g. education, health, family and mass media.

Questions 3(b) and 4(b) are essay questions worth 40 marks. Make sure you spend sufficient time on the question you decide to answer. You should therefore think about organising your ideas in the following way:

- Your introduction should define clearly what is meant by any concepts used in the essay title, e.g. 'social inequality' or 'age inequality' and should 'set the scene' for the debate by introducing the key sociologists involved in the debate.
- Outline the key theories, e.g. functionalism, in as much detail as you can. Try and illustrate key points with examples. Remember too to acknowledge the names of key sociologists whilst doing this.
- Once you have outlined the key theory (e.g. functionalism) or theories (e.g. the social construction theories of childhood, youth and the elderly), you need to examine specific criticisms or weaknesses of those theories in as much detail as you can.
- You need to examine alternative theories too, e.g. the functionalist theory of stratification could be compared with Marxist or Weberian versions; the social construction of age theories could be compared with biological, functionalist or Marxist theories of age.
- Try to construct a conclusion which comes down on one side or the other based on your considered evaluation of the sociological evidence available to you, rather than your opinion or the experience of your friends.

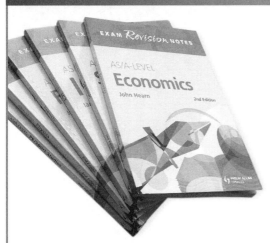